MANY HAVE PICTURES LIKE THIS

CAREY BAGDASSARIAN

Many Have Pictures Like This

IrreduciblePress

Many Have Pictures Like This
IrreduciblePress
Williamsburg, VA

Copyright © 2024 for print book by Carey Bagdassarian.
All rights reserved. Except for brief quotations with acknowledgment of this collection, no part of this book may be reproduced in any form whatsoever without written permission from IrreduciblePress@protonmail.com.

The author gratefully acknowledges the *Bellevue Literary Review*, *Hippocampus Magazine*, and *Whitefish Review*, where three of the stories in this collection were previously published.

Print ISBN 979-8-9882069-1-0
eBook ISBN 979-8-9882069-0-3

Armenian American families – Biography
Immigrant families – Biography
BIO002000 Biography & Autobiography / Cultural, Ethnic & Regional / General
BIO026000 Biography & Autobiography / Personal Memoirs

Book design and cover art by Endeavor (endeavorcreators.com)

For Julia Naz, who is the next chapter of such things

CONTENTS

An Intro by Way of a Bit of Science	1
If Not Exactly Redemption	9
Inkling	25
Immigrant Mac-and-Cheese	31
Inkling	43
Swallowing Myself	47
Inkling	57
A Theory of Longing Offered by a Scientist at Midlife	61
Inkling	81
Inkling	85
Him	89
Inkling	109
Inkling	113
Mathematics, God, or Magic	117
Inkling	141

Inkling	145
Ravens and Monsters	149
Inkling	161
Inkling	165
Requiem for a Scientist	169
Inkling	185
Inkling	189
Inkling	193
Acknowledgments	199
About the Author	

AN INTRO BY WAY OF A BIT OF SCIENCE

AN INTRO BY WAY OF A BIT OF SCIENCE

We're all looking for something. We might know what that something is; but often we don't. That's when things can run amok.

Last night I went for a walk with my friend Patty. We got to talking, about getting older, about family. Because Patty's a scientist and I used to be one as well, we dovetailed to the astounding complexity of DNA, the genetic material that's the stuff of our ancestry. You can pack in a lot of mileage with a good friend.

I remembered a study from decades ago, asked Patty if she knew it, work that struck me then as beautiful and still does. If DNA is to make a starfish or a human being, so many things have to be done to that long stretch of double helix, so many molecular interactions coordinated without a hitch.

But DNA is like a mess of cooked spaghetti scooped and packed into the cell's nucleus. In that 3-dimensional tangle how can another biomolecule find its target, the specific bit of DNA where it needs to do its work? The problem is not unlike searching for a needle in the proverbial haystack.

How does that biomolecule find its home?

Is home here? Nope. How about there? Maybe in that corner? No, No.

That molecule is also looking for something. And if what it's looking for can't be found we'd all be dead, end of story. As I said, things can run amok.

The solution to it all is what's beautiful.

Instead of a daunting search all over the place, through the entire haystack of DNA, the biomolecule plops itself down anywhere on the DNA spaghetti. Then it travels on railroad tracks, so to speak. Its quest is much simplified, the spatial dimensions of its search are reduced. No endless wandering and poking at things every which way, just travel along the DNA rails like those guys of old hand-pumping a little railroad cart. It's still hard going but at least the journey is somewhat charted. It's as if that needle in the haystack had a thread attached to it. Pull on that thread, you'll find the needle, the prize.

My own DNA tracks, literally and so much more, are those set down by my family. This collection of stories is about them. They were Armenians, all of them, my parents, my grandparents, a great uncle, my godmother. And, except for my great uncle, immigrants to this country. I've tried to skit about on their tracks looking for some target, trying to understand something of the workings of the world through their eyes. Having something of a roadmap helps.

Though everything here is based on the facts of their lives, I've fictionalized much, even a name or two, because I want to find a mythology. Why else chronicle a family's passing? Why else study the remnants of one's dead family? I guess what I'm most interested in understanding, what I need to know, is how they continued on with their lives—with their spirits intact to varying degrees—after what they'd endured by the circumstances of their origins and time and place. Their experiences weren't necessarily unique, but they were. For me, there's also the inescapable question of how I'd have fared in their shoes. Would I have emerged, if I did at all, with a petrified soul or an abundant one? And today's world has horror enough. I don't see any easy resolutions any time soon.

One of my grandmothers, my mom's mom, is only briefly mentioned here and there. She was so straightforwardly solid in her presence, there's little room for embellishment. But a few facts are worth mentioning. She was the first girl ever to receive the equivalent of a bachelor's degree in her adopted small town in Romania after WWI. As a new immigrant in the United States she immediately enrolled at night school for English. But a mortifying mishap with her dentures when reciting a phrase ended that. Maybe having to wrestle her tongue and mouth around yet another language finally proved too much. In her late eighties she confessed to me that, when she was little, she'd pray every night to die in her sleep thereby sparing her family another mouth to feed. I won't add to that. Interspersed between the longer stories are short pieces, without titles, kind of like little Inklings of something and that's what they're called. My mom also isn't featured with a long story devoted entirely to her. But she's in a couple of the Inklings. Her death so thoroughly wrung me out that I suspect most of these stories—certainly the concern in them—are really about her.

Though some of the stories seem to be about me, they come from what I've gathered from my family. I've ridden their railroad tracks for a long time. They've given me a focus, they've reduced the complexity of my search, they've done work for me. When I enjoy yet another shot of artisan espresso, I wonder if this was the future my family dreamt for me.

❧

My own kid offered to write the intro to this collection though she's only nine. I take heart in that.

Still, I had to remind her that she hadn't read any of the stories. Do you think you can do it? I asked her. Without reading them, I mean?

Well, yeah, she said.

So, what would you say? I asked. For the intro.

Just wait, she said, I'm looking for a good angle.

Okay, I nodded.

She did her fluttering hand thing.
Got it, she said, This is stuff my dad wrote.

IF NOT EXACTLY REDEMPTION

IF NOT EXACTLY REDEMPTION

My trade was in coffee, spices, cheeses, that kind of thing. I stocked six kinds of olives, some were fleshy and big, others tiny like little dried black apricots. One day a woman walked into my store. She needed rice, she said. I had plenty of that, staple that it was. Maybe the woman needed other goods as well, but it's the rice I remember.

This was all between the two World Wars. The first was done with. A second one? Utterly unimaginable. Those were prosperous times for many of us Armenians who ended up in Romania, in Bucharest. We weren't scared of hard work. I owned a car I didn't know how to drive. There goes the rich man, people said as my chauffeur drove me along in my fine green felt hat like a king.

But anyway, the woman—she needed two kilos

of rice.

I weighed it out on the old-fashioned scale. You know, the kind with two hanging pans like Lady Justice uses. We chatted. Just the usual: weather, politics, the health of Romania's king. She spoke Romanian with a bit of an accent. I was fluent in Armenian, Turkish, Romanian, and knew enough Serbian. Even a smattering of other languages. I tried each in turn until my passable Greek brought a smile to her face.

On her wrist she wore a bracelet made of marcasite that caught the light when she moved her hand just so. Her scarf was two shades of stylish red. Sometimes there's the possibility of, well, the possibility of something. A reminder that there is a Life Force, still, even after all that's happened. I wouldn't call it hope. It wasn't that, maybe it never was. But, still.

Here you are, Madam, two kilos of my most excellent rice, I said to her. Do you have all you need?

Yes, good Sir, she replied in her mother tongue, Thank you, and may God's blessings be upon you.

She paid me and I counted out her change.

I was married, two children, settled in. Mind

you, the marriage wasn't a joyous one, but it was a marriage. Devoted, yes. Joyous, no. I took my pleasure in talking with women. Wondering, as I bagged the woman's rice, how to keep our conversation going. Did she have children? What was her husband's line of work? I fantasized she'd confess to her own less than satisfying marriage. A man is allowed a fantasy, no?

With two shopping bags, one in each hand, a kilo of rice in each, she left my store. I suppose I still had a smile on my face as she walked away. What did her neck look like under her scarf? But I never strayed. Not even once, I assure you. Not entirely because I was an honorable man, though I want to think that I am. But because I was a coward. I always have been.

That night I suddenly realized I'd charged her too much. She'd payed for two kilos *and* a half. My attention had obviously been elsewhere. I tossed and turned in bed, absolutely miserable. My wife told me to go to sleep. I'd forget about it by tomorrow, she said.

But after that, every day from then on, I searched the streets for the woman. I held vigil from my store's front door. Maybe she'd return. She'd need more rice. Two kilos doesn't go very far. I would make it right. I'd give her money back. She'd accept my sincere apologies with an understanding laugh and thank me for my honesty. My wrong would be fixed.

I waited and waited for her. Of course, I never saw her again. And here I am now, an old man, in this apartment in Queens, New York. I've been here nearly twenty years, since the 1960s.

My penance has lasted to this day, a lifetime on. But how much penance is enough? How much penance is enough when the need for it started when I was a small boy?

There were ancient ruins near my childhood village. The boulders and crumbling columns were once a temple to the Armenian goddess Anahit. We kids played there all the time, battling imaginary barbarians from far off lands. Here in America, it's cowboys and Indians. In Kemah, my Armenian village, it was Mongols from the East. Everywhere, it seems, everyone needs an enemy. We drew sides and threw stones at each other. If a kid got hurt, sometimes that happened, we'd call off our troops for the day.

My older brother was the good student. My sister still too little for school. Our father had died of some sickness, I don't know what. When I neglected my schoolwork, my mother fetched me from the ruins. We'd walk back home, my hand in my mother's. My other hand holding my sister's. There were rocks everywhere, on the dirt road back home. I still feel them, their contours and menacing weight, in my small hands.

After my father died, for three or four years afterwards, my mother raised us alone.

She was still young and she was beautiful. Of course, she wanted to get married again. There were three children to feed. She needed help, a companion. A husband would bring home money. Provide for the expenses. Things anyone would want. Makes sense, no? Natural for someone left in her position, no?

My father's family didn't think so.

My dead father's brothers wouldn't allow her to marry again. They said it wasn't something that was done, good Christians that they were. They wanted my mother to stay unmarried and widowed, wearing the black clothes of mourning forever. Even though she was young and beautiful and had three children to worry about.

They took us away from her. Each of us was sent to a different house. I went to my oldest uncle's. My mother tried to see me. Of course, she tried to see me. What mother wouldn't. She'd come up the dirt road to see me.

She came once, twice. Then a third time. She'd hug me. Kiss my cheeks. She said she'd try to get me back, my brother and sister, too.

My uncle was a stern man. I didn't go to school most days because I had to work at his store. He needed me there, he said, and I stacked the goods, ran errands for him. When I had a free moment when I was not at work, I'd station myself outside my uncle's door, waiting there for my mother. I'd see her walking up the road. But after her third visit, my uncle said that it was enough.

He told me not to disgrace the family name. No one must disgrace our family's reputation, he said. I didn't understand what that meant.

I must throw rocks at my mother. That's what

he meant.

There, he said, pointing to the rubble all around. Throw those rocks.

I don't want to hurt her, I said.

No, just scare her away, he said. So that she knows you don't want to see her anymore.

But I do want to see her, I protested.

For that, I got a hard slap across my face.

I picked up a few small pebbles. I lobbed them. I wasn't aiming and my eyes were closed.

My mother called out my name, Ara.

My uncle dragged me inside the house.

This happened a few more times. I never looked when I was tossing pebbles at her. I needed it to stop. Then one day, my uncle yelled out, *Neh-deh! Hee-mah neh-deh!* Throw it! Throw it now!

She was maybe twenty feet away. The rock landed at her feet. She jumped. I broke from my uncle's grasp and ran to her.

I'm sorry, I cried, I'm sorry, Mama.

She kissed the top of my head. I earned another slap across my face from my uncle.

After that day, my mother no longer came to see me.

What little boy throws rocks at his mother? What little boy is forced to do that by his relatives? I despise that little boy.

When my wife cooks, she sings. She laughs and sings even when it's just water boiling on the stove. Even after all these years, I still don't understand how she can laugh.

Her own childhood village was, as it turned out when we talked about it, not far from mine. I met her in Romania and our marriage was arranged. Both of us orphans, both having landed in the same city, in Bucharest. We were both so young, in a new country. On our first night together, when she lifted her right breast to me, I took it as an invitation, an offering.

I had no experience with women. I moved closer to her. It was so exciting. I'd never been so close to a woman before. I moved closer still. To her. To that offered breast.

She said, Wait. Please wait. I need to show you something.

I nodded.

So you know, she said.

She lifted her breast higher and turned to the lamplight, as if the scar hidden by that breast were something to reveal and then forget once and for all. The remains of her wound were ragged, crudely healed over the years. I stared. She moved closer to the light.

When I looked to her face, her lips were pursed but she was smiling. Maybe she meant to say that it was alright. That it was our wedding night, that we were starting a new life. She was expectant, I suppose. She reached for my hand. I stepped back from her.

She was six, seven maybe, when the Ottoman Turks stabbed her in the chest. Too busy slashing at so many others to check their handywork, they left her to die. She lived, but the rest of her family didn't. When my own family was massacred, my mother and brother and sister, I wasn't there. I was in Serbia, on business with my uncle. Yes, the coffee and spice trade. We were buying goods.

I never returned to my village. Even if I could have, what was there to return to? Just rocks and ruins and the dirt roads and our stone houses now with Turkish families living in them. How my hands shook when I read in the newspapers, some years later, that the monsters who'd orchestrated the Armenian Genocide had been assassinated. I was so proud of the men who did it. And so jealous of their bravery, envious of such courage. I was impotent. I had never avenged anyone.

When I saw my wife's wound under her breast on our wedding night, healed and ragged and cruel, two inches long, well, from then on, I became timid with her. I couldn't approach her. Not in that way. She had to coax me to have children. She pleaded with me to have children. We eventually did. A son, and three years later, a daughter.

Still, in those days in Romania there was peace in the land between the World Wars. The next set of monsters was yet to come, still on the far horizon and we gave it little thought. There was little reason to see past the glamor, the furs, the respect our money earned us. You'd think we would have known. Prosperous times indeed until they weren't. Then a new monster ascended the throne. At night we dug holes in our yards and buried our gold for safe keeping. When we left Romania, all that was left behind. We lost everything.

So, here I am now in New York, New York. This grand metropolis, capital of the world. Well, it's Queens, really. But Manhattan is close enough. My wife and I have lived in this same apartment building ever since we arrived in the New World. It's where I'll die. See outside that window, past the fire escape there? Those train tracks for the subway? You get used to the noise after a while, even at night when you're trying to sleep.

Now that I have so much time on my hands, I think about these things often. The facts of my life. When my strength allows it, I still take short walks under those subway tracks, along Roosevelt Avenue.

But when I was younger? When I first came to Queens? Oh, how I'd walk. I'd walk and walk and walk under those tracks. I'd take my head and go walking. That's what my grandson would say when he was little: *Menz-heirig* takes his head and goes. That's what he called me, *Menz-heirig*; it means grandfather in Armenian. When he was little, I'd tease him with made-up Chinese-sounding words and sentences and how he'd laugh and laugh.

On my walks I'd stop at every grocery stand. A break from my thoughts, from my penance. Were the tomatoes fresh? How about the peaches and strawberries? I'd return home with bags of groceries in my hands whether we needed them or not. Then off I'd go again. The trains rumbled as they sped overhead, sparks sometimes shooting like fireworks as metal wheels screeched on the metal rails. I feared the trains would plunge to the ground. They never did. I appreciated that, that token to safety. I wondered if my hands would burn in those flying sparks.

In those early days in America the streets were filled with hippies and all that crazy hippy color. I imagined the temple to the goddess Anahit in all its glory. Goddesses and gods, women, wine and ecstasy, just wild abandon and the Life Force. Even as a child I felt that Life Force. I knew something was hidden underneath it all, beneath all the hard work and dust and the worn faces of my village, those faces that were soon to be destroyed.

And there it was in New York, the Life Force, and it looked like love beads, bandanas and bell bottoms, long hair and shorts and no bras and longing for a peaceful, colorful world. Even though I was almost an old man when I arrived here in this country, in Queens, I recognized it, the Life Force.

One day when I was walking under the subway tracks, I saw a crowd gathered around some musicians playing guitar and drumming on a wooden box. They were all singing about some kind of frog named Jeremiah. It was a funny rhythm to dance to, but everyone was singing along and swaying and twirling. My English was not too great, maybe my brain had little room left for yet another language. But I understood enough of the words, like good friend and wine. Was there anything wrong with that? The hippies just wanted peace and their music. What was so wrong with that?

You can't get too close to the gods. Your eyes would burn. Nothing would remain of your head but two charred holes. But they're still here, the gods. I know that, and sometimes they sing and dance. I edged closer to the crowd of revelers. No one seemed to mind. I swayed along with them. People smiled with me. And the chorus—Joy to the World—I understood those words for sure.

You can't get too close to the gods, but that afternoon was, for that one second, a jolt and a release until I saw in front of me my wife's scar and my mother and sister and brother. It's like that, like weighing goods when I sold coffee and spices and rice. On one side, on one weighing pan, the Life Force; on the other, the monsters. One can never know which way the scale might tilt.

My penance is not done. To this day, I take my head and go the best I can.

So, I go. Slowly, slowly under those subway tracks on Roosevelt Avenue. The trains still spark as they speed by. And their noise still rumbles in the air. They don't fall off the tracks. There are still rocks in my hand, one rock in each. I should have smashed my hands years ago. I was a good businessman, and even today my eyes can still judge produce. The coffee in America is getting better. The olives, too. I enjoy seeing children play in the parks. I'll take my head and go as long as I can. Sometimes it's enough.

INKLING

INKLING

It's such a simple thing really, the duduk, a musical instrument that's a length of apricot wood, some finger holes, and a large reed made from cane that grows along Armenian rivers. Two musicians often play together, each blowing into one. These days, the duduk makes appearances in Hollywood soundtracks. Who would have thunk it?

One musician holds a long low note, a sound like an exhale that might go on forever. The other rides above that unwavering sound with the melody, also breathy. After all, that is the inescapable nature of the duduk. The music is sometimes happy, sometimes mournful, and it's always ancient. It conjures songs to the constellations and to gods. Old wounds and much worse; loneliness and the antidote. The long note and the melody: There's something above and there's something below.

Perhaps it's fanciful to think so, but was there a low hum, a buzz, before the Big Bang, a long exhale that threatened to go on and on? Was there anticipation? Hope? Excitement? Did it sound like a duduk? Were there questions in that long-held note? Like, What will come of all this and will it be worth it?

I don't think anything is truly forgotten. I suspect we're always beholden to ancient energies and we'll always ask the same questions. And the answers? Maybe those melodies and songs of the living and dead that still ride above the primordial breath are some.

Were I able to play, I'd carry a duduk tucked away in my backpack. It would accompany me to wherever I might be going. I'd hope for a moment or two now and then to blow my own longing through a tube of apricot wood. I've held one once, the oil from the musician's hands darkening things here and there.

My four grandparents were born in Armenian villages. A few years before one of my grandfathers died, I played for him a recording of duduk music.

He listened a bit. Then he got up from his chair. He was still somewhat sprightly in his early nineties.

That's what my childhood village sounded like, he said. Then he left the room.

IMMIGRANT
MAC-AND-CHEESE

IMMIGRANT MAC-AND-CHEESE

No matter what she'd placed on the grocer's scale, a bag of peaches, freshly ground coffee, or a chunk of cheese, my grandmother nailed it every time. First she'd take a deep, exaggerated breath. Then she'd take off her glasses and wink. Finally, with her eyes tight, she'd declare categorically, "Two pounds, one ounce," or whatever weight was right. Simple as that.

To me, she was *Menz-mama*, which means grandmother. Her face and body and glasses were round. There was some hushed talk of illiteracy by the family, mostly after she was dead. And because of her shortcoming, her inability to read, my grandmother was turned away from Ellis Island when she was a nine-year-old orphan. She was already talented at needlework, she'd told us, even at that age.

Maybe the immigration officer didn't appreciate her gifts. Perhaps the language she spoke, Armenian, didn't convince him of them. The details of that encounter will remain forever obscure. But a half century later Menz-mama did finally make it to the United States, to the New World, along with the rest of us. We all came—parents, grandparents, aunts, uncles, brothers, sisters, cousins, me—all of us eager for a new life.

At the end of the nineteen-sixties, a community of elderly Armenian immigrants and their grandkids gathered each summer for a month of R&R at an old hotel in the Catskill Mountains. The men, my grandfather included, played endless games of backgammon in a cloud of cigarette smoke and thick black coffee. The women kept them alive and in clean clothes. Early every morning with a slingshot in my back pocket and a pocketknife in front, I dispatched the mandatory hellos to the old people, endured their cheek-pinches, and ran off with the other kids. Our parents were back home, working hard at the American Dream. We kids were free.

"Make sure you're back by dinner," Menz-mama, my grandmother, would call out.

We fished for hours on end, hoping for and fearing a big ugly catfish. When the winds were blowing right, our kites made mosaics of the sky. The raspberries we gathered became pies while we walked upstream on river stones, turning them over for crayfish and salamanders. Once for a few hours, we made friends with a local boy who, with his BB gun, fired five, ten, twenty shots into a long, skinny snake. They die when the sun goes down, he told us.

Menz-mama would wait for me at the end of the day on the hotel porch, sitting in a rocking chair. Her fingers busy at needlework, creating lace mandalas that were marvels of patience.

"I learned how to do this in the orphanage," Menz-mama said when I got back from that day's adventures, "I was good at it." She held up her delicate, airy work for my inspection and added, "So I didn't have to do all the cooking and cleaning. Like the other girls did."

From that rocking chair, before dinner and its dirty dishes, before the hotel's communal kitchen was scrubbed clean by the guests, Menz-mama told me stories. "One more?" she asked, and I nodded.

"Ok, then, just one more," she said, settling to the task with a nudge of her glasses up the bridge of her nose.

Her eyes stayed on her work as she told her tale. "So Aslan Haplan was at the outdoor market. He had many things to sell."

Every story was about this Aslan Haplan guy, an unsavory character who had stolen the merchandise to begin with and had a beating coming for his transgressions.

"Aslan Haplan set up a booth and everything, and a well-dressed man ... Haplan, Aslan, was selling ... the man ... evening came ..."

Every one of Menz-mama's stories unraveled. She squinted at her needlework with a puzzled look on her face as if the problem were there, in some error in her stitching.

But soon enough, she'd start to giggle. And then both of us would be doubled over with laughter, trying to catch our breath. Then another tale, and again, the giggling and laughing.

I'd once asked Menz-mama for help with my

arithmetic homework. She stared at the writing on the page, and her round face blanked over with that same questioning look. But then there was no laughter.

So, a few more stories, all chaotic and impossible to follow, and it was time to eat and we came in from the hotel porch, the tales over for now, the other families long done with their own dinners.

Menz-mama handed me a plate of macaroni piled high with a sharp cheese called *kashkaval*, her immigrant rendering of the American favorite. I loved her food.

We were the only ones in the hotel's dining room, and I had the small black-and-white TV to myself. "Just so you know," Menz-mama said in a thought-fragment out of nowhere. She shoveled more food onto my plate. "Of course, I won't be here to see it."

The starship Enterprise had just gone to warp speed and I was riveted to the TV screen. "Be here—what?"

"The world," Menz-mama said. "It will end in 2026."

She wiped her hands on her red-and-white

checkered apron and gave me another napkin to wipe my face.

I blinked and asked, "2026?"

"Yes, you need to know that," she said, adding, "Don't sit so close to the television, you'll ruin your eyes."

I let out an annoyed I-know-that whistle.

She poked me in the arm with a long wooden spoon. "What did I tell you? Don't do that inside the house—you'll call the devils with your whistles." She pointed to the dime-store print of Christ tacked above the TV, crossed herself three times, and sailed back to the kitchen.

I fashioned the last bits of *kashkaval* cheese into pellets and popped them into my mouth like tangy m&m's. The USS Enterprise battled the Klingons. For an eight-year-old kid in the late sixties, 2026 was an impossibly long time away, nothing to worry about.

And in any case, soon enough and once again forever, Captain Kirk and his crew would prove that the good guys always win.

Eventually, Menz-mama asked if I'd finished eating, she wanted to clean up. I handed her my empty plate.

Money was tight in those early days of our new life in the United States, but our fifth year gave us proud citizenship, green cards no more. While not exactly an extravagance given the scant quality of the hotel, going to the Catskills with my grandparents was an exception to our usual frugality. The three of us shared a room, and long before they settled in for the night, my grandmother first, followed later by my grandfather, I'd be deep asleep, exhausted by boyhood.

That night, as if learning that the world would end in 2026 wasn't news enough, I woke to a lamp being turned on, or maybe some disturbing sound or dream roused me. Menz-mama was naked from her waist up, undressing for bed.

Back home, of course I'd sneak peeks at my best friend's mom, chaste in a black bra under a revealing top, and that seeded my imagination of all that was tantalizing. But to witness my grandmother's huge breasts in the hotel room was a whole different landscape of fascination, confusion, arousal, revulsion, and shame in roughly equal parts.

She saw me staring, but didn't cover up.

Instead, she said, "This is where I was stabbed," and she lifted up her heavy right breast to expose the scarred flesh underneath. The wound, two inches long, was illuminated in lamplight.

"I didn't die," she added.

My grandmother let go of her breast. The scar was concealed once again.

First pulling on a nightgown over her head, she removed her slip and, after turning off the light, got into her bed.

Her mother, two sisters, and little brother were murdered. Her father had been taken from the family earlier, when they took the men. My grandmother was seven years old. She was somehow rescued, nursed back to health, shipped to Ellis Island, and turned back because she was illiterate.

The next morning, as always, as if nothing had happened, I was out the door with the rest of the kids. In the evenings Menz-mama told her crazy Aslan Haplan stories. We laughed together. Then I ate my favorite dish, steaming hot and my glasses fogging, in front of the TV.

Decades later I finally realized the obvious. With her Aslan Haplan stories, Menz-mama was reaching for the tales she'd heard as a child in her village before the world ended for the first time in 1915 with the Armenian Genocide.

I have several of her needlework masterpieces, their precision and delicacy and coherence so at odds with her stories. The thread she used on a few of them has yellowed with time. Most are in great shape. My own kid loves mac-and-cheese. But *kashkaval* is hard to come by where we live so hers is all-American. I have not told her about her family, about genocide.

Menz-mama never said just how the world would end in 2026. Perhaps she had set her sights on that far away date so that she'd be long dead when the end of the world came again. No need to live through that twice. These days, of course, I'm worried. 2026 is all too close. On the near and far horizons everywhere are fire breath and monster snarls.

I've searched online for pictures of our Catskills

hotel.

Maybe it's still standing but with a new coat of paint and much-needed repairs.

INKLING

INKLING

The red-and-yellow backyard patio was built from bricks by my parents when I was a boy. Menz-mama, my grandmother, harvested grape leaves from vines growing up the house walls and stuffed them with rice and ground meat. Back then it was my job to cut the grass. Now it was my mom's as my dad was no longer able.

My then-wife and I buried her little green parrot at the foot of a tree there. Though the bird had thrived in our sunny Los Angeles home when we were grad students there, flying from curtain rod to curtain rod, the cross-country trip and elevator-shaft gloom of the New York apartment where we now lived soundly defeated him.

I dug the hole with an old shovel that hadn't seen use in years. A shoebox coffin was dedicated to his mortal remains. But at the last minute I rushed inside the house and came back waving two plastic lunch bags.

Let's put him in these first, I insisted, unable to explain why when asked. My ex sat down on an old sun-faded lawn chair.

The parrot's bright tropical body went into a bag, and then in another, zip-locked for freshness. And finally, into the shoebox, his body padded on all sides by balled-up paper towels.

That bird drove me insane with his squawking, his sharp beak and clear disdain for me, the smart little shit. But it was a sad day.

I suppose that plastic shroud of mummification was meant to keep death from seeping into that hallowed ground where as a kid I played barefoot and climbed high trees, and from there into the house.

SWALLOWING MYSELF

SWALLOWING MYSELF

I saw her coming, her old woman shuffle bringing embarrassment my way. My best friend Dominic and I were playing catch in the street. The others—Scott and Joe, Mickey, Richard, and hopefully Janice, who hot-wired my dreams every time I saw her—were sure to show up soon. We all simply *knew* when it was time to get together. Dominic's baseball bat leaned against the trunk of a tree. Summertime and no school, a hot New York day in Queens, new mitts to break in, and plenty of vacation still left. We were not yet bored with freedom.

She was "Nasha" to me. The word means "godmother" in Romanian, one of the languages my family brought over from the Old Country less than decade ago. I didn't think Nasha was related to us by blood. But was she? Was she really my godmother? Did she dunk me in baptismal water? I had no idea. Walking down the street, Nasha looked like an apparition emerging from the heat. What was she doing here? Her hair was always pulled back in a tight bun, distorting her temples, a look you'd associate today with failed plastic surgery. Her hunched back and her limp: easy and tempting to stretch for the metaphors now, but back then none of that mattered to me. I was twelve or thirteen, and I ached for Janice. And for Diane. And I was certainly getting better at baseball. When it was my turn to go to bat, the entire outfield moved deeper.

That day, Dominic and I threw the ball back and forth. Languid, easy, highballs and lobs. Our parents wouldn't be home from work for hours, and even then we'd only be called in for dinner. Then back outside until past dark. When the others joined us, we'd ride our bikes to the baseball field with our mitts slung through handlebars, daring the balancing act of riding with a bat in hand. Just the year before, my five-speed had been stolen from the garage—until then we had no reason to lock up—but now I had a new 10-speed Schwinn Varsity, a racing machine.

Nasha lived with my cousin's family, their house about a mile's walk away. That's where she must have been coming from that day. To get to my street from there, you had to walk under an overpass graffitied with "Brahms Not Bombs" on the wall and, as commentary underneath, "Fuck You Dickhead". Pigeons roosted there, and smelling that acrid and bitter-damp pigeon-shit smell, we chucked stones at the birds. When Nasha was a ball's throw away, she waved and called my name, my actual name, not the one I'd adopted when my entire family immigrated to the United States when I was five.

"Kharen," she said.

But that didn't really matter. We were all immigrant kids on that block. We all had secret, true names mostly unknown to each other. Sometimes they'd slip out when a parent called us in for dinner. And most of us had new American names. If some of us happened to be born here, like Dominic, our parents were not. We were Chinese, Italian, Burmese, Indian, Puerto Rican, Armenian, German, Polish.

Nasha called out my name again.

And I don't know, but maybe it was that she was

impossibly old and slow, or that her thick ankles were covered in bunched-up opaque pantyhose. Or that she had walked all that way, passing under the pigeon-and-graffiti bridge in her formless old shoes that were black like the rest of her clothing, including a heavy black sweater, totally ridiculous in this sweltering heat.

Or maybe it was that Dominic was there. He was a gifted pianist and worked hard at it. He always did his homework, and he addressed his elders as Sir and Ma'am. We lived three houses apart by a hillside that banked into woods where it was rumored that high-school students got drunk and had orgies around campfires. Though we'd find the occasional spent whiskey bottle or rain-beaten porn magazine, we couldn't be certain of much else. After a few ventures, Dominic stopped coming on these scouting missions.

"What the hell does *she* want?" I said to Dominic as my godmother got closer.

"Do you know her?" he asked. "She keeps waving."

"Yeah, she lives with my aunt and uncle," I nodded and mumbled, gesturing vaguely to some place beyond the hill.

I tossed Dominic the ball and took off my glove. I set it down next to the bat. My hand was sweaty and smelled like the leather. "I'll be right back," I said and intercepted my godmother, twenty feet away.

She smiled at me.

She'd gone for a walk, she told me, not realizing how hot it was. And, lost in her thoughts, she'd walked far longer than she had planned.

From the corner of my eye I could see Dominic, the sole witness to this exchange, watching us with the baseball clutched in his throwing hand. Nasha spoke to me in Armenian, a language Dominic could not, of course, understand. The language I would have used had I chosen to speak.

When she finally stopped walking, Nasha said, continuing with her story, she took a good look around and realized she was not too far from where I lived. She needed to rest up a bit and have some water before heading back home.

I still didn't say anything.

"Can you get me a glass of water, please?" Nasha asked. "It's very hot out."

I just stood there, like stone.

"Or can you just open the door?" she tried again. "I'll get the water. Is the door unlocked?" She pointed to my house.

"What are you doing here?" I asked her.

"I just need some water," she said again. "Then I'll be gone."

"Just go home," I said.

"But—"

"I said no." I stuck my hands in my pockets.

She closed her eyes.

"You can't have any water," I said. "We don't want you here."

Nasha turned away. She walked back the way she came, down the long street and eventually she'd pass under the shitty bridge. I'd won the skirmish. But before she turned to go, she had uttered the dreadful words, "I'm going to tell your father."

I went back to where Dominic was standing, a questioning look on his face.

"I showed her," I said.

I had no idea what I meant. Dominic didn't ask.

I picked up my baseball mitt. Scott and Joe came out, then Richard and the rest. Our bikes were ready to roll. Our gloves and bats were at hand. Janice and her younger sister showed up, too, and for a while I forgot my godmother's threat. We rode to the park.

That evening I waited for my father to get home and for the inevitable phone call. Nasha would hold to her words. My father would explode with anger.

But nothing happened. We ate our dinner and chatted about our day. Then I went back outside. When I came in for the night, still nothing. Not on that day, nor the day after. I was safe. And the summer days passed as they do, always just beyond the blur of longing.

Nasha never said a word to my father.

But come the beginning of school in the fall, Dominic no longer sat with me during lunchtime.

INKLING

INKLING

We landed in Frankfurt for our family vacation, only to learn that no rental cars were available.

But we have reservations, my father and his best friend explained to the guy working the counter, a longhaired hippy dude with excellent English. My dad showed him the contract again, tapping at it with an angry forefinger, See?

The two women, my mom one of them, retreated to the waiting room. I stood my fifteen-year-old ground with the men.

My father started screaming in the guy's face, But we're Americans, we're Americans!

At that, the hippy looked dumbfounded, like he'd taken a hit. But he recovered and insisted once again, Man, we've no fucking cars here for you.

What don't you understand?

Just then, a rental pulled into the parking lot. Our enemy fairly threw the keys at us before we settled down to the paperwork.

As we triumphantly walked to the car and loaded our luggage in the trunk, my father turned to his buddy and slapped his back. And said, in the English he'd spoken for only ten years, We could have taken him, that bastard.

A THEORY OF LONGING OFFERED BY A SCIENTIST AT MIDDLE LIFE

A THEORY OF LONGING OFFERED BY A SCIENTIST AT MIDDLE LIFE

Years ago when I was a kid, my mom so much wanted a handheld showerhead to control the flow of water to her body. The hard shower stream stung her eyes, she explained over and over again. My father finally installed one in the upstairs bathroom. I was by his side helping, handing him the needed tools, a pair of pliers, some plumbing tape. My mom's immense happiness for that simple thing, that tiny concession to her need, was an infinitesimal bit of her longing satisfied. Perhaps, as a little boy, I was an old soul to have known that. But I fled from the responsibility and into stone-hard science. Maybe I simply wanted to believe in happy endings.

"Every single time I'd start working on a new one," my great uncle was saying, "there I'd be again, cursing at the universe left and right."

Before that day in the museum, I knew only that he was an artist, a painter, and that he enjoyed modest renown in Romania, his home country since the end of World War I. My mother hinted that he was also an energetic womanizer, at least in his younger years, exuberantly lazy in everything but his art, and an accomplished curmudgeon now in his old age. As a girl she had spent a good deal of time at her uncle's home. His wife, a loving and vastly tolerant woman, was very dear to my mom. Their home, she remembered, was always full with writers, sculptors, and painters. They weren't there just for the food, she insisted, I could learn something from him, she said.

My own inquiries into the Big Questions had just started that summer, right after my sophomore year in college. I was excited by my great uncle's visit. Here, surely, was a wise man come to answer those questions, an elder to reveal and revel in the great Truths. That he was then in his mid-eighties and visiting the States primarily for cataract surgery was no impediment to my quest. He'd be with us for two months—plenty of time to plunder the very core of Things.

We picked him up from JFK. My father was obsequious with the usual questions, "Are you tired? Are you hungry?" and struggled to ask them in Armenian, our mother tongue. Like my grandparents on both sides, my great uncle had survived the Ottoman Empire and that ancient language forever traveled with them. Undoubtedly exhausted from the flight, he just looked out the window at New York as we drove home. When he walked through our front door, his eyes closed as in relief to see the walls covered with his work: landscapes, still lifes, but mostly flowers.

Two days later I cornered him with the obvious as he was resting in a chair under a tree in the backyard: "What is the meaning of life?"

He shrugged that off with a flick of his cigarette and said, "That depends. What do you want it to be?"

Above my writing desk today I have a black-and-white photo of my great uncle with the writer William Saroyan. No one left in my family knows the circumstances of that meeting. There's an impish soft smile on my great uncle's face though Saroyan is fairly scowling.

The next obvious question: "Does God exist?"

After scratching his nose as if he'd never considered that one, my great uncle raised his index finger towards the ceiling. He looked like Plato in Raphael's painting in the Vatican.

"God exists," he said, wagging his extended finger to fuel his conviction.

I nodded expectantly.

"God exists," he repeated. And then added, "But I don't believe in him."

I was charged with taking him to the Metropolitan Museum. From my parent's house, the commute would involve a bus ride, a change of two subways, and a walk of several blocks. Though I hadn't thought to ask, he assured me that the trip wouldn't tax him in the least. I was, however, concerned how I'd look on the streets of Manhattan with an old man in tow. Nothing says "cool" as convincingly as a too-large NYU sweatshirt in 1980, after all.

We bought a couple of pretzels smeared with mustard from a street vendor. We sat on a bench in

Central Park. We studied street artists at their work. We went into the Metropolitan and straight to the Impressionists since I knew nothing beyond them.

Dressed in July in a three-piece suit no longer in fashion even in the Old Country, my great uncle simply shuffled, hardly pausing, from one painting to the next while muttering the painter's name. "These paintings," he said with an encompassing sweep of his beefy hand, "I know them from books, pictures."

He liked Asian art, I knew, so maybe he wanted to visit the Chinese and Japanese galleries?

He didn't answer but pointed to a small nude by Emile Chambreau. "They were almost dead by then, but I knew a few of these guys from my studies in Paris," he said, "Especially that anus-of-a-goat bastard there."

His face suddenly brightened. "Can we see the icons?" he asked. "Are there any icons here? There must be. This is the Metropolitan Museum. Where are the icons?"

There were icons. Rooms full. Endless saints, the Madonna, and Christ after Christ after Christ: from birth, to crucifixion, to resurrection in eternal replay.

"Stop slumping your ass on that bench, you're not an old man," my great uncle called from across the room. Thankfully, Armenian isn't widely understood. "Come see this one here," he said, adjusting his glasses to it.

His hair wild like the dark animal skin he was wearing, John the Baptist's bearded face emerged from a gold background.

"The gold is living, even after all these centuries. See?" My great uncle was air-tapping at the icon so vigorously, I thought we'd be thrown out.

"That's the red foundation," he explained, "under the gold leaf. It's that red that glows through." He added, "Like the heart's blood that makes you a good man, or not."

Gold, the chemical symbol of it Au. I knew its exact position on the Periodic Table, that extraordinary tabulation of Nature's elements showcasing an ordered and therefore comprehensible Universe. I remembered, correctly, the number of electrons around the nucleus. I knew that gold leaf was only a few atoms thick at most.

"Pigments are mixed in egg yolk to make the

paints. Imagine that," he chuckled, "egg yolk."

My mom has an icon at home. Its wood is worm-eaten and largely covered in a sheet of thin, tooled silver, the faces of Mother and Child peering through windows in the metal. I didn't know until then that my great uncle had repaired the icon years ago and had presented it to my mom when she was born. And that, once upon a time, he was a maker of icons as well.

"But I had to stop making them," he said.

"Why?" I asked, "Why'd you have to stop?"

"Let's go eat something first," he suggested, "then I'll tell you. I'm hungry, aren't you?"

I'm much the fan of pizza and suggested a nearby pizzeria on Lexington. We walked over and ordered a couple of slices each. "Because," he finally answered while fiddling with the ring he wore on his pinkie, "I had to become a simple man." Then he tapped his forehead twice with his index finger. "That's why," he said and shrugged his shoulders as if that were that.

I nodded as if I had understood what he meant.

My great uncle was large and his jowls hung low on either side of his chin. He had a way of resting his nose when he talked on the tips of his fingers, his hands held together in a semblance of prayer. As did so many others in Eastern Europe after the Second World War, he slept in a heavy woolen overcoat should he be escorted to Siberia. During the First World War in a much Older Country, his father died of cholera helping survivors of genocide as they staggered back from the desert. I'm here today in front of my laptop computer and second espresso because of my family's sacrifices, struggles, tenacity, and hope. A favorite line in a favorite song from my college days was "Hope you're proud of this your son."

"You know that after the War another hoard of monsters took Romania," my great uncle continued.

I nodded again, knowing the history from my father.

"Well," he explained, "they wanted propaganda posters from me."

He removed his glasses to wipe them clean with a napkin. "I told them I painted flowers mostly, flowers and trees, fruit, that sort of thing."

With his glasses back on, he continued, "And I

lied. I wasn't very good with the human form, I told them. I was a painter of flowers, that's all."

He looked away. "They believed me. The authorities hadn't bothered," he cleared his throat, "to familiarize themselves with my work."

And he added, "So you see, I became a simple man. Not even madmen can find fault with flowers."

Decades ago when his little sister, my grandmother, accepted a marriage proposal, my great uncle asked if her beau had promised her the moon and stars.

My grandmother answered, possibly disappointed, "Why, no."

To which my great uncle said, "Then marry him."

We split another slice of pizza down the middle, and my great uncle outlined the dimensions of his icons in the air. "The ones I made were never very large. They had to be portable, you understand. I'd chisel recesses in the back of the wood and set in crossbeams to protect against warping." He pointed to the fluorescent lights. "That was between the Wars. Long ago, before those things. Next, I'd apply the gesso," he continued, "a strong white base..."

"Were they hard to make, the icons?" I asked.

"Of course they were hard to make, what do you think?" he answered.

He considered his fingernails yellow with age. "The whole time making them . . . every single mongrel-abortion of a boss I ever had, donkey co-workers, lunatic girlfriends—I'd be cursing them all." He arched his eyebrows with the momentum of his tale.

"There was this one bloated-dog-of-a-mediocrity," he chuckled. "We were restoring an old painting. It was huge, that painting, and the boss put the two of us on it." He pushed his half of the pizza slice my way. "How do you stomach this stuff?" he asked.

"I just like it," I answered.

"Well. As we worked," he continued, "the bastard would talk and talk and talk. What would take two sentences to say, he'd take a day at it. I wanted to stuff his testicles down his rodent throat."

He started chuckling again, "For him especially I made up delightful scenarios. He'd be forced to kneel down to my genius because I won the Nobel Prize."

"They don't give the Nobel for painting," I, the

Chemistry and Biology double major with a good smacking of Mathematics, pointed out.

My great uncle's tongue pushed against the flesh of his cheek. "I know they don't give the 'Nobel' for painting," he said quietly.

"I just meant that..." I tried for an explanation.

But before I could find one, he rocked his head from side to side, "This world is already too full of men convinced they are right. Don't become one of them."

Had he not been certain that he was right, I wondered, how could Einstein have accomplished what he had? In those early days of my consciousness, I believed that glistening truth was to be found only through Science. I actually spray painted Schrödinger's equation on a concrete wall late at night. Today, I simply believe that all human artifacts—whether equations, symphonies, novels, or religions—are only tentative working answers to life's conundrums and mostly longings.

My great uncle touched my hand. "It is good to be young, yes?" he said and stretched to ruffle my hair. "This is the ring," he said.

"What ring?" I asked.

"The one those mediocre-dung-heaps would be forced to kiss. Like they do the Pope's."

He held the ring in his palm, studied it for some time, and handed it to me. The old silver setting held a polished dark green stone. The stone was engraved with the figure of a female warrior with wings holding a chalice.

"Have you read Dostoyevsky?" my great uncle asked out of nowhere discernable.

"Uh, I study science at college."

"All the more reason to read him," he advised me. "If Dostoyevsky had discovered relativity, it would have been 'Alyosha squared' instead of the speed of light. Less horrific, don't you think? Anyway," he continued, "I painted my icons with those insane stories of revenge going around and around in my head." His hand made circles in the air.

"I was terrified that it would seep into my work, all that hate," he admitted. "That no matter how well-crafted the icons were and how beautiful they might seem, they'd be destroyed things, vile and ugly in their spirit."

He looked up at me and removed his glasses again. "The final burnishing of the gold leaf—I'd do that with a piece of polished agate. But when I finished an icon, when I finally finished burnishing it..."

With his arms sweeping in front of him, he indicated the air surrounding us. "That hate wasn't going into my icons at all, you see," he smiled a little, but his lips were pursed. "After many years I finally understood that it was," and he swept at the air again, "just disappearing."

"How do you know?" I asked.

"Because of the gold leaf. Because when I finally applied it to my icon, all the nonsense in my head stopped. I'd be working in absolute silence, in those last wonderful, dear hours.

"But don't think the cursing wouldn't start again with each new one," he added. "Because it did—to no end. As soon as I chose the wood for it."

I looked up from my lap to his face.

"But when one was finished..." He held his hands out to me, palms cupped as if for water.

"For a moment at least, I could look at what I held in my hands and know that I made something I loved."

Death, when it comes for my mother, will find much more than a sack of used up flesh and bones. The greatest expanse of her longing remains unrequited, her soul never emptied of it. The dementia to which she's fallen traps it there.

Just today she's told me that small black stones now line the entrance to her parents' home. For her, her mother still lives. As does her mother's mother who read destinies in spent tea leaves at the bottom of cups. Whether it's any consolation I don't know, but my mother has sweetly escaped the confines of time.

Now, at my midlife, or most likely somewhat beyond, I have installed a handheld showerhead in my mom's apartment minutes from where I live. I'm praying that her dementia is another bullet she's taken for me. But there are moments of reprieve.

On a subway platform not too long ago, I saw a woman in the shadows in a red coat blowing soap bubbles and laughing with delight as the grey tunnel, scurrying rats and all, turned into champagne. When the subway arrived, and its doors opened to let her in, she chose to stay with her bubbles. I stayed behind, too, my eyes closed lest the woman become candle flame.

Several months after my great uncle's return to the Old Country, I received a letter from him. My mom read it to me, since I can't read Armenian. After the usual greetings and well wishes, he'd written, simply, "Read Dostoyevsky." And in the letter he'd included a tiny icon the size of a postage stamp. Painted on a piece of stiff cardboard and adorned with glowing gold, it was the John the Baptist we'd seen together.

Were he here now, I'm sure he'd remind me that my mother was never really longing for a new showerhead. Perhaps he'd suggest that a small inattentive breath or cough can send gold leaf floating away. Maybe he'd smile to see his ring still on my finger after all these years.

He died at home, in his own bed, when he was ninety-five years old. I felt sadness appropriate to the passing of a relative I'd met only once since leaving Romania in my early childhood. But of late, the dead and dying of my family have become my pantheon. Their stories collide in me, and it's good to know that I've been paying some attention, scant as it may have seemed to them. It takes a long time to understand your own origins.

When I'm in front of the classroom deriving the very same scientific equation for the hundredth time, I'd love it just for once to get at a totally different answer. Not because I messed up, though that is certainly something that keeps my students on their toes. Not from some inattention on my part. But because the universe, at that very moment, had whispered to its constituents, "Oh, why the fandango not?" And I overheard, just enough to slink curvature into the apparatus of science, bending its rigid ear more fully to the wild delight of the world.

In the meantime, because I am still breathing, I want to hold in my hands something I've made and that I love. Hopefully, should that ever happen, a few goat-anus-dog bastards will be around to bear witness. Longing is one rapacious fucker.

❦

In an ancient church in the old, Old Country, the

country of my great uncle's birth, there lives an icon. It was a gift from my great uncle. He made it with his hands. The Madonna's face is my young mother's. She's rendered forever in egg tempera and gold leaf.

INKLING

INKLING

She was beautiful in her nun's habit, white and black, but with stylish work boots peeking out. Thanks, she said when offered a seat on the metro, but I sit all day and it's nice to stand once in a while. Two kids scuffled nearby, their parents at a loss to control them. The nun laughed along with the children. An enormous man got on board at the next stop. Good God, a well-dressed guy let slip under his breath. I went back to my book wondering what might pass for a mystical experience these days.

I was on my way to see a collection of Byzantine icons at the National Gallery in DC. I loved icons; my great uncle had painted and repaired them and I grew up around the creepy timelessness of gold-leaf and egg-tempera saints. The metro continued along, the nun got off, the kids went on playing, and the big man finally found a seat. I kept reminding myself that this wasn't NYC, I didn't live there anymore. After my parents died, visiting NY, that city I so loved and where I grew up, wasn't the same.

In addition to the exhibit's many icons, a dozen illuminated manuscripts, both secular and sacred, were displayed in glass cases. A fifteenth-century Homer's Odyssey complimented the paperback version I had at home and showcased a long dead monk's patient work. I sounded out some words from it but not their meanings: my years as a scientist abounded with Greek letters. The lovely manuscript would fit nicely into my backpack, I thought. A large, heavily gilded icon called Man of Sorrows drew me back again and again. In almost Japanese lines of flow, Christ was rendered like a burst of waves. So, a day of gods and God, with none of the trappings. The exhibition catalogue rode heavy on my back, as if one could capture any of it in words and pictures.

INKLING

INKLING

We eased the new computer out of its box. They were huge back then: the central processing unit on the floor, the monitor and keyboard taking up an entire desk. We connected cables and cleaned up crumbles of styrofoam.

Whoa, that's beautiful, exclaimed the elder scientist, a man who'd spent months in airplanes studying cloud patterns. His brilliance and quirky personality were legends to which we all aspired.

Let's see what we got here, said the scientist who bought the computer. She pressed a button and the machine awakened with a melodious boom announcing its relevance.

Let's change the background, can we do that? asked the elder. We did, to an interesting brick pattern.

When my time came to assume the ranks of professor, I purchased the same computer for my own scientific research, by then a bit slimmer.

My interest in art and story was by then already scratching against my career as a scientist. In a rudimentary attempt at reconciliation, I used my university address for everything and my woodworking tools, books of poetry and novels, like my computers, were delivered to my office.

One day, I eased a new handmade carving knife from the Pacific Northwest out of its packaging. I sliced open my thumb. I didn't know thumbs contained fat pads. I studied the interesting ooze as blood drained from my head. Luckily, my research lab was just down the hall and my star student drove me to the emergency room for stitches. For years afterwards, I continued to practice science not to understand the workings of stars and atoms and molecules, but to breathe assurance from the steadfast logic and reliable equations of my scientific forebears.

But those four stitches in my thumb finally decided the edge on which I would live my life.

HIM

HIM

Back in the Old Country, in Romania in the 1960s, my father was recruited as an informant for what became Ceausescu's dystopic regime. I knew nothing about it, not until a fall day more than thirty years later when I was visiting my parents in Queens, New York, where I'd grown up.

"Let's go for a walk," my father said. There'd be no rain, he added, the weather report always on his mind. Lunch would be ready when we got back, my mom told us. She pointed to the clock in the hallway, don't be gone too long.

"We won't," I assured her.

My dad went to get his shoes. "Give me a minute."

Now almost seventy years old, my father was still working. By trade he was an accountant, the profession he brought with him from Romania when we immigrated to the United States when I was a little kid. When he finally did retire—the inevitable as his Parkinson's disease started to attack his sharp mind—he said, simply, "I worked for forty-five years. It's enough."

But on that crisp autumn Queens day, his mind was still intact. I settled in for the wait as he got ready for our walk. His body hadn't fared nearly as well.

His hands shaking badly, motor coordination and strength all but gone, he had successfully pulled on his shoes by the time I checked on his progress. Then began the impossible struggle with the laces.

There's an invention called Velcro, you know, I said to myself for the thousandth time.

"Don't stare," he said.

I put my hands up in apology and headed to the kitchen.

My mom had put out pita bread, feta cheese, tomatoes, and kalamata olives. There was soup on the stove. I reached for an olive, chewed its flesh, and let the pit fall from my mouth into my hand. At night as my father slept, my mom and I would stay up late drinking chamomile tea and unpacking the progress of his disease. As we did every time I visited.

He finally called out from the foyer, "Let's go."

He was a domestic dictator, a master of the arbitrary. One day your shoes had to be placed here in the hallway on the mat, but the next day that was all wrong. True, you had put them here, as instructed, but now the shoes had to be there, closer to the door, and the tube of toothpaste was to be rolled up just so, from the bottom up. No, not like that. Now, there was his disease to navigate as well and, since I lived in another part of the country, that all fell on my mom.

"You have to be a better man than I ever was," my father had told me repeatedly when I was growing up. True to his profession, he meant this largely in practical terms: more education, a more lucrative career. "The opportunities you have in this country, I never had in Romania," he said. "The freedom you have in America..." and he'd trail off his thoughts.

I got his coat from the closet. He didn't argue as I guided his arms into the sleeves but his eyes betrayed his frustration and embarrassment. With

Parkinson's, the face became a frozen mask with little expression to it, that telltale symptom of the disease. My mom and I could spot it a mile away. I said bye to her.

We started off for a long, slow walk on that crisp autumn day that needed jackets and gloves unless you put your hands in your pockets. We both opted for the latter.

From Sawyer Avenue, we headed towards Springfield Boulevard. "Now," he said, pointing to a parked silver Toyota Corolla, "that's a nice car." He took his hands out of his pockets to position them at 10 o'clock and 2 o'clock on a make-believe steering wheel. "What are you driving these days?" he asked.

"Still the Subaru."

"The black one?" he said, remembering. "The one with the stick shift?" He mimicked that motion as well.

I nodded.

"Is something wrong with it?" he asked. "Why didn't you drive it here this time? You always drive."

"It's easier to fly. Less time."

"Well, time is money."

"Yeah."

"How's the gas mileage," he wanted to know. "Does your car burn oil?"

Such matters, for him, held cosmic importance.

He'd always changed his own oil. The log he kept in the glove box chronicled his miles per gallon, the gravity of it rivaling his accounting spreadsheets at work. But now, he wasn't driving anymore at all. Another concession to the disease we never discussed, but he did say that it was my mother's fault, she put the fear of driving into him.

Does my car burn oil? "I have no clue," I said.

"It's important to keep track of these things," he reminded me. "You need to know your machine is running at its best." He ran his hands through his hair. There was enough of a wind to muss things up. He was sniffling.

I was not sniffling. With a sidelong glance, I studied his shuffling gait, that leaning forward and those quick short steps like he'd fall any second and he was trying to catch himself.

"Are you cold, Dad?"

He looked cold.

"No," he answered.

In my more generous moments I'd acknowledge the potent alchemy of spirit that propelled him into battle, day after day. From Queens to the Bronx and back again, he rode the NYC subways for the long commute to work. He wrestled those long staircases, the summer heat in the underground subway stations, the winters, the crowds, and—I'm sure of it—the obvious stares at the saliva glistening at the corners of his mouth.

"Do you want to hear a story?" he asked.

Some of his stories about life in Romania were sweet, others not so much. There was one about this kid, a classmate of his, a favorite story of mine when I was little. And that's the one he told. My father said the kid's big ears turned bright red whenever he got mad or flustered. So, he made sure the kid was *always* mad or flustered. He now flapped his own ears to make his point. Once, with the help of his friends, my father (the gang leader, naturally) hid the teacher's desk in the bathroom. Everyone blamed it on the poor guy with the big ears. Once upon a time, I would have been doubled over with laughter. Now, I just nodded as he slapped at his ears again.

We walked on, my father still believing—certain—that he could undo his decline. I will conquer this. Telling me that he'd start guitar lessons soon, why not.

At the underpass on Springfield Boulevard, speeding cars boomed overhead, their weight on the highway above rattling the concrete and steel structure. We both had the same idea at exactly the same time: Pizza. Like father, like son.

Our love affair with that NY staple began years ago when we were still new to the United States. And now, just up the road on that crisp and windy autumn day, at the corner of Springfield and Union, was the very best of it, a place called Nonni's, better than anything Manhattan had to offer, beating anything the newly burgeoning Brooklyn boasted.

"Good to see you again," Joey, the pizza guy, said when we walked in. He wiped his hands on a red-and-white checkered towel. My mom and dad were regulars, as was I whenever in town. My father headed for a table. I went to order.

Joey rang us up. "Got it, my friend. A large Margherita." He handed me two cans of Diet Coke from the fridge, said he'd bring plates over in a minute.

My dad and I smacked our lips dramatically in anticipation. I flipped open our Cokes. Our Margherita would come steaming hot from the wood oven. When I still lived at home with my parents through college, Nonni's was a tiny dive with overly greasy slices and orange plastic tables and benches. Now, it was an establishment with serious pasta dishes my father and I shunned in favor of the pizza.

Fifteen minutes later our pie was ready. A slice on each of our paper plates. Red pepper and oregano for me. Black pepper for my dad, no oregano.

"Don't tell your mother," he said, and winked.

"Nope. We'll pretend we're hungry."

We clicked our Coke cans, Cheers. But we said it in Romanian, as was our want in these situations. *Noroc*, which means good luck.

Though we were born in Romania, we're ethnically Armenian. My father rarely spoke with me in Romanian or in Armenian. We spoke English with each other. He spoke Romanian to my mom. I spoke in Armenian with her. It's hardly complicated if you've been doing just that your entire life. But for some reason, deep into our first slices there in the pizzeria, my father turned to Romanian before catching himself. Shaking his head, as in, What was I thinking?

He switched back to English and into another story from his childhood. This one was a sweet and welcome tale, a constant of our universe like the speed of light and far more comforting. Putting his slice of pizza down, he said he was on his way to school one morning when he found a little wounded bird on the road. He demonstrated how he'd cradled the bird gently in his hands, careful not to hurt the creature any more than it already was. He laid the bird on his desk at school. And that's where it rested throughout the day. But in the afternoon, it suddenly took off and flew out an open window. My dad reenacted his startled yelp and grab for the bird as it took wing.

Then he looked around. A few others—an old couple, two middle-aged women, and three high-school kids with their skateboards—were sitting to an early weekend lunch. "I need to tell you something," he said.

"Okay."

"Do you understand me?" he asked in Romanian.

"*Da, înțeleg.*" Yes, I understand.

He said that in Romania he'd been employed by a State-run company. He'd risen to a low-level management position. He was good at his job. He was quick and logical and organized. Numbers came easily to him. All that I'd already heard hundreds of times over the years, information that was corroborated by my mom. So far, then, nothing I didn't know, except the management position which didn't surprise me.

"Once a week," my father continued, "I had to go to Party headquarters." Thursday nights, he said, at eight o'clock sharp, that's when he had to be there. Every week.

The Party was, I knew, short for the Communist Party, the governing body of the State. "What for?" I asked between bites of pizza.

"When I was first called in, I didn't know what to expect." He didn't know what they wanted. But he knew enough to show up on time. The corridors at headquarters were long and poorly lit. "Not like that," and he pointed to the pizzeria lights above.

I nodded, "Okay."

"Get us two more Cokes," he suggested.

He struggled with the can's flip top, then seemed to give up on it. I opened it for him.

He leaned towards me over the table, "They told me I had to spy on my coworkers."

My father held the cold aluminum in his hand. I stared at him, my mind suddenly gone vacant, my mouth full.

His tremors swashed the fluid in his Coke can. "They ordered me to keep an ear open at work. I had to be their informant."

Anyone who criticized the boss, he had to snoop them out, he explained. He had to keep a tab on coworkers who questioned the government, anybody who spoke badly about it. The slightest bit of dissent was to be reported.

"There was no choice," he said. "I had to do it."

People disappeared, he said by way of justification. Did I know that both my grandfathers slept in wool coats? In case they were deported to Siberian labor camps in the middle of the night? There'd be no time to pack.

No, I didn't know.

Then my father smiled. "Do you remember *Rhapsody in Blue*?"

"What?"

"George Gershwin."

"Right," I said, having no clue what Gershwin had to do with anything. "You used to play it on the stereo all the time."

With a pizza slice as a conductor's baton, he took to humming the opening bars. He'd sit at the train station in Bucharest, he said, the capital, for hours. Trains came and went, and he'd hum or whistle that melody. He didn't know the composer's name. He had no idea who Gershwin was. But that music comforted him in those hard days.

"It was wintertime," he said, continuing his story. The streets were iced over and heavy icicles sometimes broke off awnings. You had to be careful. Everything was frozen that first night he had to report to Party headquarters.

Pointing to his body's midsection and then to his feet, he said, "The first thing they did was take away my belt and shoelaces."

I didn't understand. "Why?"

"Why?" my father repeated. "Because the bastards were concerned about my well-being." He said it almost angrily, as if he were disappointed in me for not knowing. "So I wouldn't hang myself with them when I went to the bathroom."

I picked at the plastic tablecloth. "So, that happened every week?" I finally asked. "I mean. They always took away your belt and laces?"

"*Da*," yeah. He wasn't the only one with stories like that, he added. Plenty of people had them. Plenty. Then he looked out the large windows that faced the residential houses across the street. The mail truck pulled up.

My dad's right hand was by his chest, fluttering, just over his heart. Pushing down with both hands on his chair, he got up after the fourth try. Those false starts before the momentum kicked in and he was able to walk to the bathroom, the son there for all of it.

Fathers and sons, they make each other nervous. And for some, there is also the trajectory of judgements and assessments—the endless do you measure up, do you measure up, do you measure up—always a two-way street and the question flying every which way.

"I played the idiot," he said when he got back, an odd small smile on his face. The front of his pants, at the crotch, was wet. He sat down heavily, scooted the chair forward to the table. The chair's legs scraped against the tiled floor.

"The idiot?" I asked. The word had a hard hammer to it in Romanian. "*Prost*?"

"I did what I had to. I reported what went on at the office." Then, of all things, he started laughing.

How could he be laughing? It wasn't funny. Was he an idiot because he thought it all was funny? Or because of what he did? Did people disappear because of him? I needed him to stop laughing.

His fingers were covered in sauce and cheese and oil. There's a saying in Armenian, usually reserved for children and hard to translate with any fidelity, that amounts to, You got what you had coming. The phrase suddenly occurred to me.

"Whatever nonsense was in my head," my father said, "that's what I told them."

I didn't follow.

He started laughing again. "I gave the bastards the weather report every week."

"The what?"

"The weather," and he pretended to shiver. "It was too cold out, I told them. We all wanted it to warm up. For the snow to melt. You know, to play soccer on the weekends. Everybody's kids had colds. Nicu had a fight with his mother-in-law. Again."

I waited for more.

"That kind of thing. That's what I gave them." He waved his hand around, as if dismissing those bastards. "Every week, they wanted to know if I had anything else for them. Something more than the weather report. *Something* had to be going on at work, they said. Didn't I have *anything* for them?"

And, Thursday night after Thursday night, he promised them that he'd pay more attention. He'd be a better spy.

"*Prost*," he said. "That's what they thought. That I was slow. Dumb. Stupid. *Prost*."

He put his slice down and picked up his Coke can, then put that back down too. He had both hands on the tabletop, palms up to the ceiling.

"I was useless to them," he said, his head askew. "Good at office work maybe, but nothing else."

We were slowing down. We were getting full. Maybe we were done. Across the street where maple trees lined the sidewalk, leaves were blowing about.

"So, what happened?"

"They let me go free."

Then he looked straight at me. He switched back to English. He reached over and put his hands on mine. "The dogs got nothing from me."

My own eyes were wide on him. As if we were little kids talking to one another about the first day of school or about a roller coaster ride or the haunted house at Halloween, I asked, "Were you scared?"

"I'd pick up my shoelaces and belt to go home. Every week until they let me go for good. I walked back out that long hallway."

Then he made a sound through his nose and his hand into a pistol, index finger out and thumb up. "I never knew when they'd shoot me in the head."

Two slices remained on the pizza tray. We'd each finished two cans of Diet. After a long moment, I got up and bused them to the recycling bin. Took the used napkins and paper plates to the trash. Got some more napkins to wipe down the table some.

"I'll take care of that," Joey said from the pizza oven, "Don't you worry." He came over with a wet wipe cloth in hand. "Looked like you two had quite the talk."

"Yeah, we did," I said, jutting my chin out at my dad. "He told me some stuff about his life."

"That's what fathers do," Joey acknowledged. "Pizza was good?"

"Pizza was good. The best."

"You want those boxed up?"

I looked at my father. He looked at me.

"Nah," we both said. "We'll manage them."

I got up for fresh plates and a last can of Coke. That one to share.

When we got back home later stuffed and sheepish and my mom at the door, she looked at us, from one to the other and back again. She said to my dad, "You missed some pizza sauce there." Then she went to the kitchen to put away our lunch.

❦

That was the one and only time my father told me that he'd been recruited as an informant for the

Romanian Communist Party in the 1960s. And that was that. Anything more about it remains stoned up in the now dead—my father, and maybe in my mother, their parents, their friends, if any of them knew.

The dim incandescent lights lining that long corridor—that I can imagine. Was the room where my father sat without his shoelaces and belt painted white and peeling? A desk or just two chairs? Did he sweat on the way out and into the Bucharest winter?

Now, so many years later, I often think about my father's admonishment. You have to be a better man than I ever was.

INKLING

INKLING

My father and I went fishing together only once. I was eleven years old, and he rowed the boat on Lake Placid while I cast my lure. We were on vacation there, just he and I, enjoying the water, eating pizza for lunch and dinner, and watching the Munich Olympics on TV.

Armed with the heaviest fishing pole my saved allowance could buy, I pursued freshwater perch weighing a few ounces. But the monsters of my saltwater dreams could fall to that gear, the pole never bending and assuredly infallible to any task. I did catch a fish.

We turned back towards shore soon after when a storm darkened the early afternoon. We'd be happy enough watching the Olympics for the rest of the day until dinnertime, no Israeli athletes yet murdered and Mark Spitz swimming his way to immortality.

As I took that struggling fish off the hook, my father, that otherwise rigid and unbending man, said, Son, you'll let that little fish go, won't you?

You'll let him live, yes? You'll let him grow up?

INKLING

INKLING

I went out for a walk late last night, Dad. I saw a spider, a large yellow and black one, strolling a foot or two above my head. It seemed to be crawling its way through the air itself. But if you moved your head just right, you could make out in the street lights the shimmer of the single silk thread. Amazingly, its ends were attached to two trees fifteen feet apart. The spider was swaying a bit with the breeze.

I don't know what happened, Dad, but suddenly it fell to the ground. Maybe the thread, stretched too far, simply broke. Or maybe the spider lost its footing as the wind picked up. I don't know which. But after curling into itself for a moment and catching its breath and bearings, the spider scurried, unhurt, across the asphalt and up one of the trees.

Like so many things these days, that spider reminded me of you.

Hey, Dad? Remember when the three of us, you, me, and Mom, went to the city nearly every weekend in my high school years before we discovered downtown Manhattan and Parkinson's disease? We'd first go our separate ways, then meet up again at that bookshop on 50th to enjoy the day together. That's right, it was a Brentano's. Mom window-shopped at Saks. You liked that sporting goods store. That one near the 53rd street subway, remember? You'd study their tennis rackets without ever buying one. It became our joke, that soon they'd lock the doors when they saw you coming. I miss your laugh.

MATHEMATICS, GOD, OR MAGIC

MATHEMATICS, GOD, OR MAGIC

A day like so many others as my grandfather called from the backyard, "The helicopter's here!" My grandmother's call back from the kitchen window, "Did you give the signal?" My grandfather's answer always, "Yes, I did. I gave the signal."

The smoke rising, as it did on so many days, fragrant and oily, to the Los Angeles sky. And once again, satisfied that there was no fire, the pilot banked the helicopter away.

My grandfather would follow its trail until it vanished, waving a greasy piece of cardboard at the sky. Then, his attention back fully to the barbecue, he'd fan the coals and turn over the fish.

He was much younger then, my grandfather, but still an old man.

A good share of his very-old-man days also passed outdoors in his backyard near the foothills of Griffith Park. He'd hold up his plastic wine glass for another swallow. "This vine here, see this little vine?" he asked. I'd put down my book and join him.

My entire family called him "Tata," which of course means Father. The man wrote his own eulogy—refining it over years and years as death continued to pass by him, but not his friends and not my grandmother—and he signed himself off the planet with that name, simply as Tata.

"Look, Kharen, look here, my son. How does this little vine work its way along the tree's branch, winding itself so perfectly along it?" he'd ask. If that vine hadn't captured his attention, it'd be a visiting skunk, or hummingbird, or once, to our amazement, a nighttime coyote with the neighbor's cat dead in its jaws. Tata pointed a bony finger at the living green helix.

"And how does it jump from the branch to the fence, to continue its brave journey?" He'd gently touch the vine to follow it along the now dead plum tree his wife, my grandmother, had watered and pruned for years. We all loved the jam she'd make from its fruit. The tree died two months after she did and it's wrong not to find some sort of significance in that.

But with a slow shake of his head Tata would add, "Why did this plant ever seek out this old fence?" as his finger touched that too, that tension of life against metal, like his hand on his aluminum cane.

Perhaps because he respected me as a Man of Science—those were his words—he'd ask of me as much as of the vine, "What mathematics lies behind it all, what secret logic pushes this bit of life so assuredly on its way?"

I was on sabbatical leave back then from the university in Virginia where I taught chemistry and I'd come to Los Angeles, using it as a base for travels, research, and writing. A free place to stay at Tata's, plus potent memories of California's mountains, deserts, and my graduate-student days at UCLA. It was good to be back.

To be honest though, the sabbatical year was largely a midlife attempt to breathe after divorce. I'd put my stuff in storage, loaded up my car, and headed west. Tata was zeroing in on ninety-five years of life, his fire and questions undiminished. Each time I drove away from his house for some roaming I wondered if he'd be around when I returned. He was, and so was the vine. I needed to be near him.

"Can it be mathematics?" he'd ask again, countering my silence.

My memory yielded only dim recollections of mathematical models for growth hormone distributions in germinating plants. But before I'd have a chance to suggest anything cogent, my grandfather, now squinting up at the sky with another pull at his wine, would wonder, "Or is it God?"

I'd met a woman in New Mexico during that year and was going back for another visit in a week. Sex was simultaneously tantalizing and terrifying, as it must be for all not-so-young-anymore men wildly aware of their less-than-stellar performances in life and love. Still, neither God nor Mathematics had a chance against this woman's beckoning. The relationship didn't last. "I don't know, Tata," was the best I could offer.

To this confession, he'd nod his head, reminded once again that the overly educated haven't defied ignorance either. His own formal schooling ended at the sixth grade. "We'll never know, will we?" he'd conclude with a shrug of his age-shrunk shoulders, which did little to defuse the urgency of the issues at hand, his and mine.

But before I could nod my own head in reluctant agreement that we'd never know whether Mathematics or God fueled life, he'd amend his prior musings with a third possibility: "Or, in the last analysis, is it magic?"

He could drive you nuts.

The universe would not, I sensed, tolerate the fast vying against the slow. There was, of course, the usual deceleration as I found myself braking to Tata's pace. Food was chewed clear to a liquid before swallowing. Windows and doors were carefully secured against very dangerous drafts. Tata suspected that my laptop computer monitored our conversations. All matters of importance, especially that one, were therefore discussed far from its electronic reach. Luckily, his clandestine calculations revealed that the distance from the living room to the kitchen sufficed as long as you whispered. Such things make it easier not to turn the man into a god with the passing years.

So: Mathematics, God, or Magic? There'd be no easy answers, neither for grandfather nor grandson. But there'd be food.

After donning tie, jacket, and trench coat (a fantastically lengthy process but you never know whom you might meet and it's often breezy out), we headed to our favorite Armenian restaurant after one last trip to the bathroom. Tata pointed to a table in the shadows and there we sat. And as soon as the waiter walked off with our order, Tata reached into his coat pocket for a smuggled plastic water bottle.

Swatches of its decaying label still clung on, and I saw that he'd fitted a cork into the mouth. "I'm just an old man," he explained in singsong as he opened the bottle and snuck a first taste of wine. I retreated to the artwork. On the far wall was a painting of a bejeweled Indian woman with Kamasutra-worthy breasts immortalized on black velvet. Abandoning any pretense to decorum, Tata called to the waiter for an empty glass and some ice, which he got without reprimand, a concession to the very elderly, I supposed. He filled the glass halfway with wine, added the seltzer water that he'd ordered, set his improvised wine bottle on the table, and kicked back a little. He had nothing to hide. Often he'd share his stories with me. But not now. I glared at him as we faced off in subterranean silence.

Until, finally—salvation. A small meat and bulgur rice dish brightened with tomatoes and onions for Tata. Hummus, olives, pita bread, and Diet Coke for me. We were ultimately two simple men. And with a toast to the ceiling and whatever else might hover beyond, Tata invited his wife of seventy years to join us before we dove in to chew and chew.

Some things in this world are categorically clockwork. Like our simultaneous grab for the check and his promise to let me pay when I was his age. And the fifty percent tip.

"Tata, that's too much," I said as always. "Just leave less." Either way, it'd be fine since the check usually hovered around twelve dollars max.

"I could," he agreed with that shrug of his shoulders. "But generosity is what spared my life."

Yes. Generosity, graciousness, and grace in dimensions of which I am absolutely incapable. And luck, too. To the end of his life, he'd wake screaming in the night. Sometimes in Romanian. Sometimes for his mother, this always in Armenian. Most often for things I haven't earned the right to tell. But the language of his nightmares articulated the memories he was revisiting.

Tata was a master alcoholic, never even buzzed. Like a time-released drug, his watered-down wine irrigated his demons throughout the day in measured sips. Only once, as far as I know, did he miss his mark. He got more animated that one afternoon, a bit louder. That's all. Talking about nothing in particular. Nothing ugly or embarrassing. But I ran my car into the back of a pickup as I fled north on the freeway.

We finished our meal and he set down his empty glass. He wiped his mouth. He opened his eyes big behind his glasses. And with his ancient hands held palms up as a makeshift weighing scale, Tata once again juggled the three options laid raw before us: Mathematics, God, or Magic.

Just the other day I read that coyotes regulate their numbers. Too many? No problem—the females have smaller litters. Too few? Litter size just pops back up. Try to kill 'em off and they'll just throw it back at you. An irony Tata, now dead three years, would have appreciated.

I informed my wife Liz about this discovery. "Yeah, makes sense," she said immediately.

"It does?" I asked. "How does it make sense?"

"Well, when there's a lot of coyotes they can't be well fed. Some of the embryos probably just starve."

"That's not how it works," I retaliated, miffed at her quick and thoroughly plausible explanation.

"OK, so how *does* it work?" Liz asked as she reached for the TV remote. Her exasperation was ultimately forgivable. But first we had to persist to the crystalline truth.

Lacking any keener explanation than the one she'd given, I just opened up my hands and wiggled my fingers in the air. But Liz knew me and asked from the couch she'd plopped down upon, "OK. So how do you *want* it to work?"

"I, uh, well, maybe when a female coyote yips and barks, she keeps track of how many yips she hears back. And, then, well, she figures, There's a lot of 'em out there, I better, uh, keep it under wraps."

Completely ignoring my conjecture, she said, "Cats can be impregnated by more than one male when they're in heat." Liz has had experience with this feline phenomenon. But I reminded myself that experience was no substitute for endless debate. "You think coyotes do that too?" she wondered.

Stumped again, I related for the tenth time my favorite real-life coyote sighting a few years back, the one with Tata. In the spirit of good storytelling, however, the tale was revised this time to feature a very scraggly coyote, like it'd been sucked through a vacuum cleaner, but, man, was it big and the cat ever bloody.

"I'm gonna call Sandy. She'll know all about this coyote stuff," I informed Liz, who'd escaped to the kitchen. Sandy was a biologist.

"Sandy? Do coyotes regulate the number of pups they have by keeping track of how many other coyotes are out there and adjusting their litter size accordingly?"

"I study amphibians."

"Yeah, yeah, right. But do they?"

"Do they—how would they do that?"

"I thought you'd know. Even though you study amphibians."

"What was the question?"

I elaborated and enunciated thusly, "Maybe coyotes can, I don't know, act accordingly. Like cranking it down when there're too many. Population control, you know."

Sandy exhaled, "Accordingly to what? They're probably not as well nourished and so have smaller litters. What's the big deal?"

Next I called Jen on her cell phone. She was a mammalian biologist. She studied mammals, I mean, not that she herself was a mammal, which of course she was. Oddly though, I got her husband instead. That'll do, I figured; the guy knew some ecology. So I asked him, "Can coyotes, you know, control the number of pups they have?"

Probably because it was getting late, he suggested, "Can't you just Google it?"

"I thought you'd know about coyotes."

"You called Jen," he reminded me. But being a good man, he answered my question. "When coyote numbers decline, more nutritional resources per coyote become available and the mothers can sustain larger numbers of developing embryos. You want me to put Jen on?"

"No."

A brainy childhood friend of mine once speculated that humans of the future would evolve humongous heads perched upon useless bodies. He seemed genuinely excited by the prospect. Which now reminded me of the Chapman brothers sculpture, Übermensch, in which Stephen Hawking sits atop a craggy rock formation in his iconic wheelchair. He's reaching for the heavens but also precariously close to tumbling off. Neither my friends nor Liz have particularly humongous heads nor useless bodies, I assured myself.

On the way to teach class the very next afternoon I heard a crow call out again and again a common West African drum rhythm: Caw - - caw - - caw - - - caw - caw. Where'd it learn that, I wondered before realizing that maybe it was the other way around.

After more than a decade of teaching, it's become increasingly wracking to come up with something important or interesting to say. "It's a tough job to explain the meaning of life when you have no idea," as the writer Jim Harrison has it. My students shuffled to their seats. Armed with a few minutes before the start of class, I wandered off to the bathroom. Where, steadying his hands at the mirror, a student prepared to inject a syringe of conductive goo into his electronic headwear. Kind of like an old Cronenberg film, gruesome and funny.

"Psychology experiment?" I asked, pointing to the glorified neoprene swim cap complete with chin strap and dangling Christmas lights. "Yup," he answered, "we're gonna map my brain patterns when I'm asked embarrassing personal questions." Thoroughly encouraged by such forthcoming revelation, I replied with a hearty "Ah" and went to teach. Indeed, the paths to knowledge are myriad and wonderful.

Everything we're learning about atoms, I told my first-year chemistry students, everything about molecules and their reactions is just one of many stories told to make sense of the world. It's stories that propel us and maybe that will always be the case, I stressed.

You see, I continued on, embellishing an old joke, after many, many years of toil by many human minds and hands, the world's most powerful computer was ready. It was absolutely huge and had been built solely to answer that One Question that's hounded us from the very day our brains evolved enough complexity to be hounded. Those responsible for the machine's creation wiped their brows, shook hands, and patted each other's backs. "Good work, good work," they said.

And—finally!—the moment of truth.

Team Leader, the ultimate brain behind it all, stepped up to the computer. He flipped the power switch. The machine, startled to awareness, buzzed and clicked and whirred into being. So much so that everyone jumped back. "Ha-ha," they laughed to steady their knees. "Ha-ha."

Team Leader approached the computer again and touched its face panel, his hand lingering. "This is the most powerful and intelligent computing machine ever created," he explained, though all present obviously knew that. "Let's see what my baby can do!" He fairly blushed. And sidling up even closer to the machine—which whirred and buzzed with its own anticipation—Team Leader prepared to ask of it the One Question.

"Computer?" he demanded above the electronic chatter. And, above the chatter, lo, an answer. A "Yes," not at all robotic, but almost soft and sage.

Gasps of appreciation all around. More back patting, more shaking of hands.

And then, with Team Leader's breath moist on the machine's shiny skin, his fingers seeking out a knob, the Question:

"Computer, what is—what is the meaning of life?"

Everyone leaned in close for the Answer, waiting, waiting. Buzz, cling, whirrr. Everyone leaned in closer, closer. Until, until: Zzahh! The machine paused for an eternal moment. It cleared its electronic throat.

And then, finally, in an almost velvety voice, it revealed the Answer: "Let me tell you a story..."

The word that comes to me most when I think about my grandfather is "holy." Not that he was, but he relentlessly looked for it everywhere and in everything. The danger in coming off the familiar north-south-east-west grid—whether intellectually or spiritually—is that you can lose your mind unless you make music with all that's thrown at you. Tata never found rest from the question "Mathematics, God, or Magic?" Of course he knew it was all three—Mathematics and God and Magic—and also none of them, and that was the problem. Or, more accurately, he tried to live his life at their confluence, the place of story.

He once told me, "You know, when you were little, people thought of you simply as my grandson." I nodded my head at the obvious. "But now," he continued, "they just think of me as your grandfather."

For the fifth morning in a row he'd called me to the kitchen. I closed the door behind me as he'd asked. My eavesdropping laptop was to overhear none of this. The discrepancy, he explained very calmly, between his actual birth date and that on his passport—he tapped at it with his finger—was *still* troubling him. I rolled my eyes. For two decades he'd been anticipating some terrible consequence born of this error and for two decades we'd been hearing about it. My grandmother, when she was alive to suffer his concerns yet again, would instead just go outside to her flowers.

Why he didn't correct the mistake when the passport was renewed was a question he'd forever evade answering. Again and again, Tata hushed me to lower my voice as I explained for the zillionth time that nothing would happen; that the government didn't care; that his birth certificate was lost in some tiny Armenian village almost a century ago; that no one paid attention to ordinary people like us anyway.

For five days we'd had the same conversation. I tried these same attempts at rationality—*nothing will happen*—for five days straight. That morning I lost it. He begged me over and over to stop yelling at him. Anything I write now would betray the howled screech that finally escaped him as he grabbed his head in his hands to escape my assault.

Friends ask if I'll ever write down Tata's stories. But they're not mine to tell. As I said, I haven't earned the right to tell them.

Liz and I like to take walks at night. Near our home there's a small lake, human-made for the neighborhood but delightful nonetheless. In summer it's lush with reeds and home to many critters. Great blue herons hunt along its edges. We walk to the lake often, though she insists I leave my phone behind.

Tonight a vigilant dog blocked our path there.

But pretty much anyone would finally relent to Liz's soothing assurances and the dog was no different. It was hot, early June, and the frogs were simply out of control.

Some sang in absolute synchrony, holding the same beat, others responded with interjected staccato calls. Bullfrogs groaned the bottom to add the needed funk against the altos and tenors. Something like "Oh yeah" but undoubtedly far more complicated. On past nights, we'd been able to count out individual frogs.

The lake's utterly nonhuman life could sometimes shake me of the world's infantile madness we stupidly call human nature. But not tonight. "Or more like human nurture," I started in, getting ready to elaborate with my usual nonsense. Liz put a hand on my thigh and said, "Baby-love, let's just listen to the frogs." She was right. We had a frog riot going here.

Sperm whales sing to each other in clicks. The structure of their collective communication—a cacophonous jabbering is what it sounds like—had long baffled scientists and remained opaque to mathematical analysis. But on an inspired hunch, a Senegalese master drummer was invited to listen to whale-song recordings collected off the Canary Islands. After identifying the number of sperm whales, thus confirming the scientists' only conclusion, the drummer tweezed out each whale's contribution and the song's dominant beat as established by one particular individual. When asked how he'd known all this, he said simply, "I don't know how, but I know."

Liz knew that story. I'd repeated it to her a dozen times after reading it in David Rothenberg's *Thousand Mile Song*, and she was likely waiting for my inevitable analysis of the frog music. The discussion had so many obvious ports of entry: What kind of frogs were these? How many were there? How did they synch up their calls? How many songs did they sing? Were they actually mating? What were they saying to each other?

We sat listening to the frogs. The occasional passing car hushed them, but they quickly forgave the intrusion and returned to their singing, their urgency unabated. A cat strolled by silently as only a cat could, possibly thinking, I was worshipped by the ancients, I am revered by the moderns.

I turned and waved to a driver though I couldn't see inside the dark vehicle as it passed. Just reassuring everyone that Liz and I were decent people even though it was late, and this compulsion to do so—as though we were somehow suspect or suspects—made me angry. We mean no harm, I wanted to scream. We just like frogs. Who, now that the car was gone, were again indifferent to the human world. Our skin gathered the night's moisture.

Liz met Tata only once, when he was three months from death. Wildly unshaven, still six feet tall though sunken, his English dismal after having lived in this country for decades, he didn't quite inspire Liz to jump into his arms for a grandfatherly hug. Too many years in the desert eating too many locusts, that's what he looked like. He did, though, take her head in his hands to kiss her forehead with the immense hope that fed his life, his family's, and so much more.

As an older man, Tata had made a pilgrimage to an ancient church sacred to his ancestors. The stone stairs to the altar were many and he climbed them on his knees as was the custom. When he returned home, a friend asked if he'd gone to pray for something or to give thanks. "This time," Tata answered, "this time it was to give thanks." I should have told him, leaning close to his ear, "I need you."

We sat listening to singing frogs, Liz and I.

I tried to imagine him here now, the three of us pondering Tata's One Question as he did throughout life. "Tata, come sit," I would say. He does. Somehow he's brought a newspaper to spread on an old bench that didn't exist a second ago. His back isn't any straighter or his limbs looser. Death doesn't suit him.

But there's his plastic wine bottle, uncorked and ready at his side, and a plate of feta cheese and slices of pita he's carefully set out on the newspaper. Some baklava, too. He nudges the food towards Liz, knowing I'll help myself without encouragement. As a stern warning to us though, he shakes his finger at the wine before taking a swig. Liz reaches first for a piece of baklava and then for the cheese. With his hands and chin resting on his cane nestled vertically between his knees, Tata nods in approval.

We finish up our snack and settle into the frogs. Tata seems so tired, as if the return to gravity has compounded the exhaustion of being dead. His eyes blink, his only movement. But he seems to be listening. I want to open the floor to discussion, thinking that it'll fire him up to talk about all those crazy frogs. Why's he so quiet? Is something wrong? Maybe he's not feeling too good?

But before I can say a word about the frogs or ask about his postmortem well-being, Tata puts a silencing finger to his lips. "What's the matter..." I start to ask.

He just shakes his head with a tiny smile, his finger still there.

The frogs sing.

Let us, something whispers to me, let us make no further comment but allow time to ripen such humid-night mystery into unassailable words.

INKLING

INKLING

Your stitching isn't bad at all, my grandfather Tata said to me. With the hands and eyes of a connoisseur, he ran his fingers along the edges of the leather satchel.

For a living he had made and repaired Oriental rugs, as they were once called, a trade he'd learned seven decades and four countries ago. He nodded appreciatively at my efforts until he hit an uneven stretch. I told him I hoped to sell my bags one day. He closed his eyes in slow consideration.

So, he said, you've studied all these years to become a scientist, a professor, only to end up working with your hands like a laborer?

I hardly expected that.

He pressed on. This is why we came to the United States? For you to get calluses on your fingers instead of staining them with ink?

I just want to make satchels, that's all, I protested, and added something sarcastic about computers instead of fountain pens, the modern world, you know?

He disappeared into the back of the house and returned with an armful of box cutters, hammers, awls, scissors, a pair of pliers with the grips covered in rubber tubing. Take what you need, he said as he laid the tools of his craft out in front of me.

INKLING

INKLING

Deep in the night, the old scientist, old of both age and of time, set his quill down and capped the inkwell. Had the sky cleared? He fetched his telescope from its leather case and opened the doors to the balcony. But still no planets, and even the moon was bereft behind clouds.

No matter.

When perfected, long in the making and pages upon thousands to create, his mathematics would track the progress of heavenly bodies through the sky even if his eyes couldn't. How long did he have left? A decade? Two? If his health obliged, perhaps time enough. Pulling off his shoes and britches to get into bed, he once again rehearsed his address to the Academy.

Colleagues and friends, he cleared his throat to

say, the astonishing and hidden logic of the Cosmos is finally revealed to us . . .

And as he settled into sleep, he shivered with the thought that his equations might also track that hidden God whose presence had receded ever so infinitesimally, a bit more each day, since his childhood long ago.

RAVENS AND MONSTERS

RAVENS AND MONSTERS

Here are some things I so much wanted when I was an immigrant kid just starting school in New York: no weird last name, no strange foods, no big noses, and my parents' broken English gone forever.

"You're an American," my dad told me repeatedly back then. "An American boy of Armenian heritage, but you were born in Romania," he'd say. To cement the American part, I insisted that my mom pack white-bread bologna sandwiches in brown paper bags for my school lunches. I became a serious student of Star Trek. I learned to recognize the makes and models of the muscle cars dominating the roads in those days. Still, a teacher once referred to me as the kid with the funny last name.

The facts were embarrassing enough. What to

tell my friends? That my grandparents survived the Armenian Genocide of 1915, and they ended up in Romania? That we left Romania with nothing in our pockets when I was four or so and lived nearly a year in Beirut before immigrating to the United States? That in Beirut my father made a little money teaching a bit of English to dozens wearing exactly our shoes? When I was in the fifth or sixth grade, for reasons I don't remember, Romania came up on the evening news. I was mortified. No, it wasn't embarrassment. It was shame. My friends would surely have seen me and my family as losers. My people were massacred. I was born in a communist country, that black-and-white personification of evil that America fought in the Cold War.

I read scores of books about the Holocaust in graduate school. Though I was drawn to the extraordinarily powerful literature, yes, I was also sidestepping the weight of my own family's story.

Later, I found ravens.

I love those birds. They're so crazy and strong and exuberant in their tumbles and spirals. The sky is their servant. When they're on the ground they do that comic bird hop, so at odds with their elegance in the air, but even those terrestrial maneuvers are assured and muscular. Ravens would so crush it in a gym.

Once upon a time in the Cascade Mountains, I heard one calling with a soft, musical ah-ooo. The rain had just stopped. The fresh afternoon sun was out. The mosquitos weren't quite crazy yet. I scanned the trees for the bird. Another seductive ah-ooo narrowed my focus.

Was the raven talking to me? I sure hoped so.

There it was, the bird perched high in a standing dead red cedar. I reached for my binoculars. The raven flapped its wings once, twice. Then it realized I was there. I put the binoculars down. The raven groaned, that change of talk when they know you're staring.

I circled the cedar for a better look, angling for a clear line of vision through the tree's bare branches. Then, from my vantage as I looked up, the sun aligned directly behind the raven's head. And the raven's translucent black beak was illuminated to an astonishing blood red.

Some years later and farther north, just south of Fairbanks, I watched nearly forty ravens eat away at a dead caribou in a snowstorm. The carcass was white, the ravens getting there, too.

I've also seen them hanging around dumpsters in Southeast Alaska harbor towns. The ravens thinking what? That they're freakin' seagulls? Their feathers can get so out of sorts. I don't know, perhaps it all fit in with the monstrously huge cruise ships and tourist-trap Alaskana knick-knacks fucking with the cloud-covered meeting place of mountains and forests and sea.

"What's wrong with you?" I said to the first raven I encountered in that state of disrepair. I was within five feet of it. Its indifference to me was total.

Just then, its buddy flew by with what looked like an entire chocolate doughnut in its beak, somehow chattering as it went. I aimed my phone for a picture of the first raven but it flew off.

Maybe a meal is a meal, you know?

❦

In the Pacific Northwest it's often a short step from ravens to Raven, the trickster and cultural hero of indigenous cosmology. For me it was. After all, wasn't that sun-beaked raven that I'd seen really a glorious reenactment of *Raven Steals the Sun*, performed just for me? And dumpster-diving ravens? Raven the mythbeing, too, was not above stuffing his face. So, yes, a short raven hop from bird to Raven—especially if you're trying to escape your own culture and stories, something I'd been doing my entire life.

Nearly a century ago, my great uncle had honed his chops and paid the bills as a young artist by painting icons in the Christian Orthodox tradition. He depicted saints, Madonnas and Christs in all manner of pain and ascension. The icons adorned with gold leaf, their haloes and backgrounds glowed with it. I turned away from that iconography to one of Bear and Eagle and Killer Whale and, of course, Raven. I fell in love with Pacific Northwest art and stories. I learned all I could. I went to Alaska and British Columbia often to marvel at the land and masks and totem poles. I took to carving wood.

After all, if bologna sandwiches, Star Trek, and muscle cars can transform an immigrant kid into a full-blooded American, then why shouldn't a few carving knives and an adz or two turn a grown man into a woodcarver working in traditions not his own?

Since then, I've learned that you never really escape your own story no matter how many years pass and how far you may travel. I've a raven to thank for that knowledge as well.

On the last day of another trip to that same Alaska town, the one with the disheveled ravens but years later, I walked along a road that followed a waterway. The tide was out, and the exposed beach was covered in kelp and rich with mussels and all sorts of shore-stuck sea creatures. Every raven in town was invited to the feast.

They poked and pecked at the bounty left by the forever dialogue between sea and moon. Just ravens doing what ravens do. I wondered if they, too, like the rest of us, searched for a small but perfect arsenal with which to understand the workings of the world. In any case, here was a moment of raven redemption as they ate something other than doughnuts.

Off to the side, though, was a very large one.

It was bigger than the rest, totally gnarly and lording it on a piece of driftwood. The other birds shied clear of that raven and, even to my human eye, it looked to be insane.

"You're Armenian and were born in Romania, but now you're an American," my father had said again and again when I was growing up. "We came to this country to have a better life, to leave all that behind," he said. Some members of my family came with open hearts; others arrived with souls damaged by what they had endured. But all worked hard. All of them. My parents made a life for me.

Staring at that raven, at that sinister bird, I suddenly realized that my father had been wrong about that very last part. We had a better life, an unimaginably better one for which I am forever grateful. But you never leave anything behind—no matter how far you think you've come, even to some distant Alaskan shore to the land of the totem pole.

Much more than economic opportunity, the American Dream was for my family, once and for all and forever, the final escape from fear, terror, and annihilation. A few years before he died, my mom's father, Tata, had said to me over a glass of wine and feta cheese and olives that we'd finally have peace when the whole human race becomes a homogenous brown color. Then there'd be nothing left to fight about. But that menacing raven said otherwise.

It said, We'd still find things to kill each other over. There will be strife, always. The world doesn't lack for monsters. As I've said before, there are always new ones on the near and far horizon and, always, fire breath and snarls.

My flight back home from Alaska was early the next day. I took leave of the ravens and walked back to town and to a coffee house I liked. The espresso there was not too bad, and it was a good place to sit, think, write down ideas, and read after hikes and excursions. I'd been doing just that for two weeks.

I took off my rain jacket and hung it over the back of a chair and sat down at the table. Espresso in hand, I opened up a book and absently read a page or two. I slipped the book into my backpack. Writing didn't much go anywhere either. I snapped closed my pack's buckles. Usually I'd be sad to be leaving Alaska. This time I was ready for home.

After twenty years at it, I don't suck as a woodcarver. I still love the art and stories born from Raven. But that trickster belongs to another people. These days I look at a lot of Armenian art and play around with gold leaf. But that necessary and essential tension between chaos and order—ravens eating trash and ravens in the sun, entropy and emergence—I'll always crave.

It takes a long time to find a trickster of your own. I'm still looking for one of those. That work continues.

INKLING

INKLING

Tanked on doughnuts and espresso, hard rain outside, an American flag across the street, absolutely lunatic in the hard wind. I close my laptop, sick and anxious with the world's news. The café is tight and tense with college students. Final exams start tomorrow. A pregnant woman walks in, sets down her wet umbrella and unzips her raincoat. A purple tee-shirt hugs her prominent navel.

After finals my own first semester in college, I walked the eighty blocks from Washington Square to the steps of the Metropolitan Museum. A straight shot up Fifth Avenue, twenty blocks to the mile in NYC. For a good ten minutes I hopped up and down the steps singing I'm done, I am free, I'm done, I am free. Soon enough, the students studying here in this café today will be called upon to perform.

Why bother? I want to ask them. Semester after semester, again and again. Can't you see what's going on out there? But that's hardly fair. It's their time now to learn that poetry and mathematics are both thinly disguised recitations of fire.

Nearly missing its perch, it's so windy out there, a crow lands on the flagpole. The bird's throat looks like it's struggling to dislodge hell. But when the pregnant woman opens the door to leave, pausing to sweep her umbrella upwards (such a beguiling, simple act), I hear the crow cry out its defiance against the wind and rain. And so it goes, this balancing act of wild rejoice and dark realities.

INKLING

INKLING

Scotch and overheard conversation fill the quiet places of the poem I'm reading in dim light. I listen to the night flirtations between customers as they preen for words that promise to deliver. There's a request for another beer. One bartender asks the other, Did he really just say that to me?

Rinsing glasses, pouring a draft, calling in a food order, she's a fire of hair. The guy she's now chatting with is sweet on her. He slips his phone back into his pocket without her number. I admire the well-worn messenger bag slung over his shoulder, a bike lock looped at his side, the astonishingly large black ear studs that don't simply happen overnight. A cheer goes up at a touchdown on the TV screen. I read another stanza surrounded by stories, our true anatomy and physiology.

The slow-burn poem conjures high school sweethearts and dead fathers, including mine. And, soon enough, speculations about my own death.

When? How? My daughter?

I eat a handful of peanuts to shake myself of these old-man things of life.

Because in the last silent spaces uninhabited by words, liquor, and women, the poet's making good on a promise to himself decades old: Me, I want to make work that doesn't lie.

REQUIEM FOR A SCIENTIST

REQUIEM FOR A SCIENTIST

They're all dead now, of course, all of them, my parents and grandparents and my great-uncle who made icons decorated with gold leaf to beat back his demons. I'm still here. Once upon a time my family called me a man of science, for that was what I had been, and my last act as a scientist coincided with that of spawning salmon. Standing in hip waders in an ankle-deep stream, I nudged at a dead sockeye. Spawned out as they say.

Patty, my dear friend and co-instructor, was helping our students with their dissections. One of them offered, her head thrown back up to the sky, the most amazing seagull imitation. Such longing there was in that heartbreaking human-seagull cry. The hair on the back of our necks stood up.

Do it again, we all insisted. Then back to work.

We harvested six fish. A quick sharp blow to the head and death before surgery. A salmon's immune system resides in the spleen and kidney, and Patty's research has contributed greatly to understanding salmon health. Our students were learning about that. My role was to address the salmon's place in the larger ecosystem.

Co-teaching is never easy for college professors. There's enough ego and one-up-man-ship to sink the Titanic. Did you *read* that scathing and *scintillating* piece in the *Atlantic* augmented yet brilliantly *decimated* by you-know-who in *The New York Times*, name drop, name drop, name drop?

It helps to love the person with whom you're teaching. Then the class might work. Straight-jackets the egos somewhat. It helped, too, that our course—christened *Salmon Tales,* a title Patty and I were proud of—took place in Alaska, on the Kenai Peninsula, at Quartz Creek, Moose Creek, at Skilak Lake, in fast flowing streams with salmon near the end of their days.

So, seven students, Patty, me, with salmon and dozens of seagulls wheeling overhead, drawn to the excitement but too wary to land. We'd always leave them offerings of fish guts.

Their iconic red bodies and green heads aside, spawning sockeye salmon aren't a particularly pretty sight. Covered in fungus, the males sporting hooked jaws and Halloween teeth, the females somewhat less hideous without the hook, salmon at this stage of their life cycle—the end of it, that is—are beyond what humans can eat.

Still, as ugly as they are to our human eyes, the fish that escaped being sacrificed to science got it on even while drawing their last gasps of water. The males fought. Females defended their nesting sites. They released their eggs; the males, milt or sperm. The little bright red-orange balls got fertilized to give the next generation of salmon.

Biology majors that they were, the students already knew a good deal about the salmon's life cycle.

I pointed at a female who'd just chased off another vying for her territory. You know that these fish were born right here in this same body of water, I asked.

Yeah, the students said.

When they're big enough they swim downstream out to the ocean.

The students nodded their heads.

Only to return from the ocean a few years later. Then they spawn and die, right? Like they're doing now.

Uh-huh.

But the students didn't know that salmon literally starve themselves. Once back from the ocean and in freshwater leading to their spawning streams, salmon don't take in any food. And *that* after surviving orcas and seals and sharks and bears and waterfalls and dams and being turned into sushi.

All for what? I asked.

Silence.

Why bother? I demanded. Why just spawn once, just once, and die looking like shit? I swept my baseball cap at the drama around us. They're masochists, these freakin' fish, you know that?

I interpreted Patty's look as somewhat encouraging.

So, I said, putting my cap back on, Why bother?

To ease our guilt for killing six salmon that we couldn't eat and denying them the chance to breed, we'd mix the eggs and milt of our harvest hoping for the best.

As a graduate student at UCLA years ago, I spent a lot of time on my bicycle. My family was hardly aware of my extracurricular activities. They envisioned a very noble me poring over books and manuscripts, late nights in the lab, coffee stains affirming the intensity of my work which threatened to steer the Earth clear from its very orbit, so brilliant was I, their man of science.

Before that, I'd satisfied for a whole year my family's dream that I become a physician, the paragon of job security and status for immigrant kids. You'll always have work, my father advised me, his only child. I was kicked out of medical school. From New York I fled to LA, from cadavers and flesh to the mathematical side of things, into theoretical science. And the amazing bike rides.

Whenever we could, my buddy Paul and I hit the roads. We loved the high deserts, the Angeles National Forest, all that chaparral and yucca trees and hard climbs and fast descents. Once, on a midnight ride, the only light that of the full moon, we were chased by wild dogs but out sprinted them.

Paul turned to me afterwards and said, totally deadpan, Quantum mechanics doesn't work out here, dude.

He'd meant it as a joke, of course, but there was something there. Those clean, crisp, beautiful (though maddeningly hard) equations and theories we wrestled with as students and, later, as scientists, sometimes bore scant relevance to the issues at hand. Standing in those Alaska waters three decades on, the toes of my hip waders nudging at a spent, dead salmon, I considered the Why Bother of things.

You get pulled into it all, staring down into the stream and your own one-day-coming-for-sure death though I was fairly sure our twenty-year old students didn't see it that way. Paul's invocation seemed rather relevant.

Can you come here and help some? Patty called out to me. Everyone was at work, all hunched over their dissections.

It's hard to look busy when you're juggling the infinities. I had to forgive Patty for not realizing that's what I was doing. So, Uh, yeah, I said. I took leave of my dead salmon. I cleaned the dissection pans, scouring them of blood and guts and bits of flesh with little pebbles and sand from the stream.

When we were back from our field work each evening, we detailed the salmon food web and the energy flows therein. I introduced the Gaia Hypothesis, the idea of the Earth as a self-organized complex system with its life forms working in tandem with the planet's oceans and geology and atmosphere. I suggested that the immune system, all those networks of molecular interactions that Patty had discussed, was a molecular-scale model of network dynamics on the planetary scale. I was that man of science my family once applauded.

There's an astonishing transformation mask made by the Haida artist Robert Davidson, and I showed our students an image of it pulled from the internet. The outer face is that of a spawning sockeye salmon, hooked jaws and teeth and vibrant orange-red and black paint on carved red cedar. A tug of a rope and the dying salmon's head opens wide down the middle by way of pulleys and hinges to reveal inside the next generation, a young new salmon head, a celebration of rebirth.

And, back to the question: Why don't salmon eat on their return journey up rivers and streams? Why starve? Why bother?

Because fasting salmon—food for bears and wolves and ravens and eagles—also feed the trees.

We talked about the science of it; about the tons and tons of salmon biomass bringing energy to streams without taking anything from them; about isotopic ratios of nitrogen and phosphorous, the scientific sleuth work proving that the trees have a molecular signature like that of the ocean where the salmon grew big and strong. Salmon flesh feeds the trees' wooden bodies, and so the entire terrestrial ecosystem.

Good work, people, I told our students. Good work.

Then I flashed a poster by Roy Troll, the familiar image of salmon leaping up a waterfall. But the artist had rendered hearts all around and a caption. Salmon: The Fish That Dies For Love.

It's not a very long jump from the science to the metaphors of Gift Giving, Sacrifice, Rebirth, giving your flesh for the benefit of another, the Hero's Journey.

You throw a ball across a field, it comes down, no ands, ifs, or buts. Thanks to Isaac Newton you can write gorgeous equations to calculate the ball's parabolic trajectory. Those same equations govern planetary motions and the arc of ballistic missiles and the physics of my once fast bicycle descents down California canyons. There's grounding and steadfastness and sometimes comfort in those equations and in all physical truths—in the facts of things, the biology, the chemistry and physics. Predictability remains the scientist's bread and butter, chaos theory and all that notwithstanding. As a scientist I'd found meaning, too, sometimes, in physical truths. And if not exactly meaning, then at least a surety.

It's the metaphorical truths that are by far more slippery. They're the realm of the gods of old, of mythtime, dreamtime, psychology since the 20th century. Though we've largely banished the gods from every day, maybe, just maybe, their ancient energy lurks, a bit muddled and suspect to be sure, underneath all our longing and anguish and triumphs and defeats. Like when we need a different kind of meaning. Like when we ask, Why bother?

I told our students that Hermes, the Greek trickster god, didn't eat the burnt-flesh offering he made to the other deities. Oh, he wanted to, but he wanted more to be accepted by Zeus and the rest as their equal; to grow his stature in their eyes he had to stay hungry. And the mythbeing Raven, a gluttonous fellow if ever there was one, refused food at one point in his journey. He needed something other than a full stomach. I left it to the students to make the jump to the many spiritual traditions practiced by humans.

With dying salmon at my feet, I was surrounded by stories of Sacrifice and Gift Giving and Rebirth and the Hero's Journey. With that last one, though they're all often inseparable, Disney makes a killing movie after movie.

Something must die if something else is to live, of course. That's the food web. But it's somehow also how we see the workings of the world and perhaps why we make so many mistakes and why we're often so monstrous. It's as if biological necessity has become our entire cosmology. If I'm to live, I must eat. If I'm to live, you must die. If my beliefs are to live, yours can't. If my gods are to survive, yours must be destroyed.

From where do our stories come, those that floor us and feed us? I nudged at yet another dead salmon.

I'm convinced there is an invincible need in our souls for these ancient and necessary concerns. Still, even today, in this late date of the jaded. Did our students care what a man several decades older had to say? I didn't know.

So, we harvested salmon. We did science. We talked about stories. Fast trout called Dolly Vardens darted about every which way, they love eating salmon roe. People catch them on fly rods with their favorite food rendered in bright red-orange plastic.

❂

Our last day in the field with salmon. The students would be flying home tomorrow night.

I wasn't quite ready to be back in Anchorage, though I enjoyed the coffee houses. Even in Alaska, there's someone who can't shut up. Oh, look at that tree there, that spruce, I think it's a blue, no, no, a black spruce, and, oh, that contrail! Must be coming from Fairbanks, last flight of the day probably, but it's so pretty here let's just be quiet a moment and take in that little waterfalls. Wait! Is that a mountain goat? Can you see the International Space Station at night?

But we had one more day off the beaten path with our *Salmon Tales* course.

Everyone by now was adept at removing spleen and kidneys and drawing blood. Even bludgeoning salmon over the head had become, keeping with the nature of humans who get used to anything, a matter of course. But a student did remark that he'd seen the eyes change when salmon died and that had him thinking. There was a bit of a drizzle and plenty of raspberries in the bushes around the stream, wildly sweet though you had to keep an eye out for bears while foraging for the treats.

One more salmon to dissect, last one of the day.

A student picked up the freshly dead female sockeye and was about to run a scalpel through flesh. A slight pause.

The student put the salmon back down and made a funny little smile and motion through the shoulders.

Yeah, well, the student said. Uh, yeah, right.

Are you okay, we asked.

Yeah, yeah. I'm fine.

Then the student picked up the salmon again.

And looking at her face said, Thank you.

Then, one by one, each student knelt down.

One by one, each said to the salmon, Yes, thank you.

And so it was.

INKLING

INKLING

When my mom was healthy and young and very much alive, she said that if she ever got sick, something terrible like cancer, she'd take the express train out. As a New Yorker, she much preferred skipping all those intermediate stops, the subway creeping along, Let's go already, for crying out loud.

But she missed the express. Those doors opened and closed way too fast for her to get on.

Near the end of her days one morning, she took a few sips of water through a straw. On the table next to her were black-and-white photographs of the already dead. Her mother and father, her husband, the aunts and uncle who loved her.

Though she sipped water, my mother once again refused to take food. As she had on our flight from the Old World to our new life in this country, when she didn't understand that the food offered her was free. She tried to explain to the flight attendant that I should eat, that I was hungry, she herself didn't want any food.

Sitting there with her at her deathbed, so many years later, I wondered if she again did it for my sake.

INKLING

INKLING

Such a weightless thing, the dragonfly was brilliant indigo in the sun. But it landed on my car's antenna with gravity enough to set it in motion.

I loaded up for a last run to Goodwill. Clothes mostly, I'd deal with the furniture later. From the parking lot, I looked up at my mom's third-floor balcony.

Three years ago, a pair of barn swallows had made a nest there in a corner. They flew at their task all day long and my mom repeated incessantly that birds were extremely intelligent. Just another annoying byproduct of aging, I guessed, but I was proved wrong as her dementia progressed.

The nest now remained only as a splotch of mud. I considered the flowerpots, weeds growing in them, and the two outdoor chairs and table I'd forgotten about. It'll never end, I thought. I'd kept two dresses my mom had made for herself. Her jewelry I'd give to Julia Naz, her granddaughter, when she was older.

A swallow suddenly perched on the balcony's black railing. It did a quick hop the way birds do. It crooked its head towards me. We studied each other for a very, very long time.

When I finally stepped away from the car for a closer look, the swallow flew off. They're so fast.

I started the engine. The dragonfly took flight as well. The long metal antenna vibrated. Would the swallow hunt down the dragonfly?

INKLING

INKLING

I gathered them together in my heart the best I could. My grandparents. My great uncle the icon maker. My father. My mother. She was the last to die.

I imagine we're at a coffee house, the line at the counter is long, mostly locals, and I have us in Anchorage, why not, at SteamDot, my favorite. I take my place in line to order coffee for my family. But my father taps my shoulder and insists we get some pizza first.

So off we go, across the street. How's the science business going, he asks. Well, you know, I say, and we leave it at that. My father and I share a whole pie while my grandparents and my great uncle and my mom are happy with a thin slice each. Satisfied, we return to the coffee house for hot drinks and pastries.

My mom floods her cappuccino with a ton of sugar. And, pointing to my espresso, she asks as she always does how I stomach such bitter stuff. I shrug an I-don't-know. Austerity on my part and luxury on hers, the usual order of the things of our lives reversed. We click our cups together and say the Romanian word for cheers, *noroc*, which really means good luck.

Outside, a young man passes by the window. Severed far above the knee, his left leg is a short stump. Suddenly, he twirls a crutch high above his head, and through the window we hear him singing as he hops away on his one remaining leg.

My grandmothers clear our table, wiping it clean, and vanish back into death. My grandfathers and great uncle, still discussing the politics that had consumed their lives, join them. With a salute my way, my father says that he wants more pizza and another Diet Coke and he disappears into the light rain outside.

Do you need another espresso? my mom asks me. She's leaning against the window, still watching the one-legged guy dance down the street.

I say, Yes, sure, thank you.

Ok, I'll be right back, she nods, But then I have to go, too. She waves vaguely at the firmament and goes to order.

She puts down the hot cup in front of me. She offers me half her brownie. She touches my hand. Our family's work isn't yet over, she tells me, But you know that.

Then she vanishes.

ACKNOWLEDGMENTS

Writing is a craft. You get better at it by working hard. And you need people who read your work, who are honest with you about it.

To those who've been honest with me, who have helped me push on, my utter gratitude. Gene Tracy, another scientist who took to the writing road. Maggie Almdale and Dave Waskin for our continuing work together. Rick Bass for so much and the sage advice, No work is ever wasted. Matt Holloway, for his keen ear and encouragement. Patty Zwollo and Chris Pallister for their friendship and for Alaska year after year. Joanna Lee, my student years ago and a far better writer than I am. Teresa Longo and Kelly Crace, thank you. Elizabeth Mead, visual artist, for our work together on Inklings. Antonia Fowler, the last reader of this collection and her verdict was a relief. Elizabeth Wiley suggested an audiobook version and introduced me to Steven Jay

Cohen, whose narration is spot-on perfect. Charlie Morse, though he jokingly insisted that an Armenian with a very strong accent should have read the audiobook instead, always had faith in my writing. My uncle and aunt, Navasart and Maral Kazazian, have been massively supportive—I hope not just because they're not in it though Navasart's parents and sister and uncle are. Maral introduced me to Sahak Ekshian. He and Refined Eye Inc. created the cover art for the ebook version of this collection. Grace Khoma of Endeavor designed this book, cover art and all.

Thank you, all of you.

Him was previously published in the *Whitefish Review*; *A Theory of Longing Offered by a Scientist at Midlife* in *Hippocampus Magazine*; and *Mathematics, God, or Magic*, with a couple of minor differences, appeared in the *Bellevue Literary Review*.

And last and foremost:
To Julia Naz, I love you, kid.
Finally, to Elizabeth, with more than I can ever say.

ABOUT THE AUTHOR

Until not too long ago, Carey Bagdassarian taught at William & Mary and over the years his work has taken him from science to interdisciplinary studies to writing stories. All three are good things, often similar, often different. Though he's written a story called *Requiem for a Scientist*, he's discovered that, like family, like one's ancestry, very little is actually left behind. His stories have appeared in the *Bellevue Literary Review*, *Hippocampus Magazine*, *Whitefish Review*, *Leonardo Electronic Almanac* (MishMash), and *The Trumpeter: Journal of Ecosophy*.

www.ingramcontent.com/pod-product-compliance
Lightning Source LLC
LaVergne TN
LVHW041250080426
835510LV00009B/670